little books for

BUSY MOMS

Kids' stuff
and
What to Do
With It

Resources from MOPS

Books

> Beyond Macaroni and Cheese
> A Cure for the Growly Bugs and Other Tips for Moms
> Getting Out of Your Kids' Faces and Into Their Hearts
> *Little Books for Busy Moms*
>> Time Out for Mom ... Ahhh Moments
>> Great Books to Read and Fun Things to Do with Them
>> If You Ever Needed Friends, It's Now
>> Kids' Stuff and What to Do with It
> Loving and Letting Go
> Mom to Mom
> Meditations for Mothers
> A Mother's Footprints of Faith
> Ready for Kindergarten
> What Every Child Needs
> What Every Mom Needs
> When Husband and Wife Become Mom and Dad

Books with Drs. Henry Cloud and John Townsend

> Raising Great Kids
> Raising Great Kids for Parents of Preschoolers Workbook
> Raising Great Kids for Parents of Teenagers Workbook
> Raising Great Kids for Parents of School-Age Children Workbook

Gift Books

> God's Words of Life from the Mom's Devotional Bible
> Mommy, I Love You Just Because

Kids Books

> Little Jesus, Little Me
> My Busy, Busy Day
> See the Country, See the City
> Mommy, May I Hug the Fishes?
> Mad Maddie Maxwell
> Zachary's Zoo
> Morning, Mr. Ted
> Boxes, Boxes Everywhere
> Snug as a Bug?

Bible

> Mom's Devotional Bible

Audio

> Raising Great Kids

Curriculum

> Raising Great Kids for Parents of Preschoolers *Zondervan*Groupware™
> (with Drs. Henry Cloud and John Townsend)

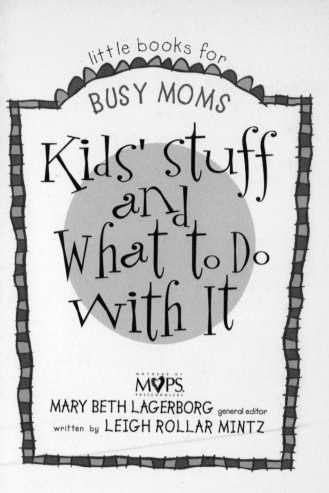

little books for

BUSY MOMS

Kids' stuff and What to Do With It

MOTHERS OF
MOPS.
PRESCHOOLERS

MARY BETH LAGERBORG general editor

written by LEIGH ROLLAR MINTZ

ZondervanPublishingHouse
Grand Rapids, Michigan

A Division of HarperCollinsPublishers

Kids' Stuff and What to Do with It
Copyright © 2000 by Leigh Rollar Mintz

Requests for information should be addressed to:

🏛 ZondervanPublishingHouse
Grand Rapids, Michigan 49530

Library of Congress Cataloging-in-Publication Data

Mintz, Leigh Rollar.
    Kids' stuff and what to do with it / Mary Beth Lagerborg,
general editor ; written by Leigh Rollar Mintz.
       p. cm. -- (Little books for busy moms)
    Includes bibliographical references.
    ISBN: 0-310-23511-1 (softcover)
    1. Storage in the home. 2. Children's rooms--Planning. 3.
Children's paraphernalia. I. Lagerborg, Mary Beth. II. Title. III.
Series

TX309 .M55 2000
643'.1'083--dc21
                                    00-043292
                                         CIP

Published in association with the literary agency of Alive
Communications, Inc., 7680 Goddard Street, Suite 200, Colorado
Springs, CO 80920.

Interior design by Melissa Elenbaas

Interior Illustrations by Thomas Ungrey

Printed in the United States of America

---

00 01 02 03 04 05 /❖ DC/ 10 9 8 7 6 5 4 3 2 1

To Cameron and Collin,

my two precious gifts from God.

Being your mommy is the best thing in the world.

Contents

Help for Busy Moms

I LIKE TO STUDY moms in the grocery checkout line, moms with a child in the cart grabbing at the tantalizing gum and candy displays. Usually these moms don't resemble the women posed on the magazine covers next to them. These women are on a mission: to feed and care for their families while at the same time teaching their children to make good food choices, to not pull things off the shelves, to not whine, and to stay close to the cart. No matter what their size or shape or age or education or experience, they're trying to be the best moms they can be.

To be the best they can be, moms solicit advice from parenting experts and mothers and grandmothers. But sometimes the best help of all comes from other moms who, traveling the same road, have made some great discoveries they're willing to pass along. Thus the series Little Books for Busy Moms was born. We've chosen topics to meet the needs of moms, presented in a format they can read quickly and easily.

One thing moms need is help to keep from drowning in the clutter of all the stuff that accompanies life with a child. Leigh Rollar Mintz believes that organizing a child's stuff helps the child as much as it helps the mom! She tests her organizational theories and tips daily on clients through her business, Let Leigh Organize, and at home with her two active sons, Cameron and Collin.

Here is a treat just for you, Mom. You can enjoy it in little bits and pieces or all at once. We hope that, in little ways or large, what you find here will make a lasting difference.

MARY BETH LAGERBORG
PUBLISHING MANAGER,
MOPS INTERNATIONAL (MOTHERS OF
PRESCHOOLERS)

Personally Speaking

UNTIL I BECAME A mom, I never realized how much babies need and how much stuff kids accumulate—it can be overwhelming! Like most mothers, I struggle to find enough time in the day to get everything done, and I simply can't waste a lot of time searching through clutter for the things I need. It didn't take me long to realize that the only way I could avoid constant chaos at home was to create a variety of organizational systems to keep all my kids' things under control. Now, as a single working mother of two young boys, I realize more than ever before how much the three of us benefit from the order that results simply from organizing all our stuff.

When I was a child and was asked what I wanted to be when I grew up, the only answer I ever gave was "a mommy." Then, when I actually became a mother, I felt my deepest desires had been satisfied. I loved staying home with my baby and fulfilling my role as wife and mother. I enjoyed doing the little extra things for my family. Unfortunately, my marriage ended several years ago, and I had to make some hard decisions about my life. The most frustrating and painful thing was the idea that I would no longer be a stay-at-home mom. Out of my desire to be with my kids as much as possible, I thought about starting a home-based business.

After much soul-searching and prayer, I asked the Lord what talents I had that would enable me to start a home business. He spoke clearly to me: "Organization." As crazy as it may sound, I've always loved to organize stuff. My world just seems more peaceful when all my things are in order. As a mom, I believe that my children feel the same sense of peace and security when they always know where to find each toy, book, and article of clothing.

My business got started when I helped my friend Anna get her home in order. She was thrilled with the results and suggested I help several of her friends get organized. From there, Let Leigh Organize continued to grow just by word of mouth. My clients *love* having order in their homes! When they experience a newfound sense of control, they gain the motivation to maintain and continue the process.

Of all the complaints I hear from moms, the most frequent one is about all their kids' stuff. Both parents and children feel chronically frustrated when their homes are messy and disorganized. I am truly convinced that the assurance of order in their homes gives children comfort and security as much as it gives parents serenity and control.

The Lord gives each of us special talents, and I believe he gave me the talent of organization to share with other moms like you. I also believe he gave me this gift because of my younger son, Collin.

God knew I would need an abundance of organizational skills to raise a developmentally delayed child. I realized this fact at one of Collin's year-end school meetings. I was surrounded by those directly involved in Collin's educational guidance and teaching. They told me that Collin had progressed so well during the year that he would mainstream into the regular school program the following year. They also said that his developmental delay was related to his struggle to "organize" his movements and thinking. My first thought was about how important it is to Collin to have all of his things organized and in place. Of my two boys, he is the one who thrives most on order at home.

When I was telling my girlfriend Misty about Collin's teachers' report, her face lit up. She said, "That's why God chose *you* to be his mommy." Misty believes Collin has overcome most of his developmental problems because of the structure and order I have provided for him at home. I can't tell you how wonderful that thought made me feel. I truly believe that teaching our children about order benefits them far more than we realize!

I hope this book will help you learn some easy ways to bring order into your child's life. When your home has order, it inevitably has more peace, and yet, the greatest benefit will be to your child. When you create special places for your child's things, you make your child feel special. What a wonderful gift!

Acknowledgments

To MY HEAVENLY FATHER, who is truly the author of this book, for I have learned that it is only through you that I can accomplish anything. Thank you for loving me unconditionally and using the painful times in my life to strengthen me.

To Terry Willits, thank you for believing I could do this. You have been an inspiration to me in so many ways. Thank you, too, Bill, for advice on all the legal matters. My heart is filled with joy that Bailey was brought into your world.

To Beth Lagerborg, thank you for all you've done, and especially for your kindness in walking me through the bookmaking process.

To Carol Howell, my editor and angel on earth, thank you from my heart.

To all the wonderful people at Zondervan Publishing House, thank you!

To my clients, thank you for allowing me to come into your homes and unleash my creativity. I appreciate your trust in me.

To Andy Stanley, and North Point Community Church. Thank you for the blessing of such awesome teaching and being part of such an incredible church home.

To Keeley, Liz, Sue, Kathy, and Anna, thank you for being such precious friends. I appreciate and love you all. Keeley, you have been my rock.

To my fellow single moms, Misty, Pam, Kathleen, GiGi, Laraine, Trish, and Rebecca, I love you guys! It is so encouraging how much we support each other. You mean the world to me.

To my mom and dad, thank you for all you've done for me. My words of appreciation may not have come as often as they should have, but know from my heart that I love you both very much. Cindy, thank you for loving me as if I were your own. To the rest of my family, Bobby, Sheila, Bobby, Jimmy, Anthony, Tommy, Gary, Debi, Gary, Rachel, Rick, Amy, Heather, and Zachery, I love you all.

To Glenn, a man after God's own heart, thank you for your love and support.

And to all the moms out there: always remember that you are a gift to your child and the Lord chose you specifically to be your child's mommy.

"Let us not become weary in doing good, for at the proper time we will reap a harvest if we do not give up."

GALATIANS 6:9

CHAPTER 1

Giving the Gift of Organization to Your Child

IF YOUR LIFE IS anything like mine, you sometimes have a hard time keeping your head above water. Sometimes I find my plate overloaded with so many difficult things that I look up to God and cry "enough already!" Especially in times like these, I look to him to calm me down and reassure me. I have to admit, though, there have been days when it took awhile for me to hear his message. But he has been patient with me.

I want to share with you a very personal and embarrassing story. It happened about two weeks before my book was due. After a very long and tiring day of organizing houses, running to meet the kids' school bus, supervising homework, a rushed dinner, and baseball practice for my son, we finally made it back home around 9:30. Both kids were dirty, tired, and cranky because it was already an hour past their bedtime.

After I got Cameron and Collin cleaned up and in bed, I walked into the kitchen and was greeted with a sink full of dishes, snack-littered counters, and a pile of laundry on the table. My bedroom looked even worse. I was exhausted and knew that I had hours of work to do on my book. I was so tired and discouraged I just sat down at the sink and started to cry. I cried louder and louder and called out to God in despair. In my frustration, I began carelessly tossing pots and pans into the cabinet without any thought to the clattering sounds that resulted—I was completely and totally overwhelmed.

Apparently, Cameron heard all the noise and came downstairs to check on me. I'm sure it was scary for my son to see me "lose it." I had never lost my composure so completely, and the whole scene upset both of us. Cameron was frightened, and I was even more upset than before because I had unwittingly drawn him into my feelings of hopelessness.

Fortunately, I managed to calm down pretty quickly and reassure him that everything was really all right, but the episode that night was a learning experience for me.

I realized that if I took just a little time to put things back in place, I would feel better. It worked! In only fifteen minutes, I got my house back to relative order. I know that there are times when my emotions make me feel like things are worse than they really are, but that's another whole book! The key to my getting everything back in order was organization. I had a place for everything.

But what would have happened if I hadn't already made a place for everything? If that had been the case, fifteen minutes wouldn't have made a dent in the mess, and I would have felt completely out of control. As it was, my frustration was short-lived. This experience gave me new insight into the feelings of a chronically disorganized person when she faces clutter day in and day out. And when I think of the children of a disorganized person, I have to ask myself, "How do they feel?"

If you bought this book, you already have the *desire* to get your home and your child organized. That's the vital first step! This book is loaded with ideas to help you through the process. I would like to share with you some ways in which children benefit when we, as parents, help them to become more organized.

- *It makes them feel secure.* A child gains a profound sense of security when she knows each of her possessions has an assigned place and that she can count on finding the things she needs.
- *It makes them feel special.* When we make special places for his things, our child receives the message that he is important and special to us. Children take great pleasure in knowing special places are created in the home just for them.
- *It teaches them to be responsible.* When a child is taught to keep his possessions in order, he learns valuable lessons about becoming a responsible and dependable person. When he is taught how to accomplish these tasks and then shows responsibility by performing the tasks without direct supervision, he feels proud of himself.
- *It teaches them appreciation for all God has given them.* When a child is taught to take care of his things, he gains more respect for his possessions and more appreciation for his parents and the many other blessings in his life. When

he learns to appreciate his own things, he is more likely to be considerate of the possessions of others.

- *It prevents frustration and confusion.* When a child knows where to find his things and knows where to return them, he is far less frustrated in everyday life. Not only does an orderly home reduce daily stress for your child, it also brings less chaos and more peace to the entire family.

- *It helps them be productive.* When a child does not have to waste time searching for his clothes, his toys, or his school supplies, he is able to accomplish more in less time.

- *It makes them feel they are a vital part of the family structure.* When a child realizes that she is responsible for some contribution in the care of the home, she feels she is a vital part of the family.

- *It promotes good hygiene.* By color coding or otherwise designating which personal items are for the exclusive use of each child, you eliminate confusion over what belongs to whom. Illness will be better controlled if your children are not sharing toothbrushes, washcloths, or drinking cups.

- *It teaches confidence.* When we have high expectations for what our children can do, we give them confidence in themselves. Too often, we rob our children of feeling successful by taking care of things for them. Have confidence in them, and they will be more confident children. Furthermore, if your child perceives that she is capable, she is more likely to set higher goals for herself.

- *It encourages more playtime variety.* When your child's toys are organized, he will be able to see what is actually there and will play with a wider variety of toys. Easy access to creative tools such as markers, drawing paper, and craft kits will help develop artistic skills; shelved books at kids' eye level will encourage reading; neatly stacked games and activity toys stored within sight will be enjoyed more often. Keep toys visible, and they won't be forgotten.

- *It can be lifesaving in emergencies.* Organized family emergency plans can save the life of your child in a crisis situation.

- *It provides a foundation for the rest of their lives.* When a child experiences consistency and routine at home, he develops a sense of structure that carries over into school life and beyond. The examples we set and the lessons we teach our young children have far-reaching effects. We are laying the foundation for their future.

These are some important reasons for us to keep our homes organized! Whenever you feel completely frazzled, stop and remember *why* it is so important to have order for your children.

Each child is unique and will benefit from organization in different ways. It can be quite discouraging to work really hard at bringing order to your home and feel as though your child hasn't learned a thing. Don't give up! Children always learn from their parents—we are their models! So even if you think that getting organized is a wasted effort for your child, try to remember that he *is* learning, even if it doesn't seem like it.

My son Cameron is a good example. He is the creative-messy type, and his room can get quite scary at times. I would like for his room to be more orderly, but it's *his* room. When I do ask him to clean it up, it shocks me how quickly he can put everything in place. He does a really great job! I have taught him lessons about order, and he has learned from me even though he isn't naturally inclined to be neat. Have faith that your teaching will pay off!

One word of caution ... don't expect to have a perfect child, or to be the perfect parent. Such an objective is impossible and will inevitably lead to disappointment. So, don't be obsessed with neatness, just make a consistent effort to minimize clutter.

If you have made the decision to bring more order to your life, set realistic goals. It's tough to change old habits, so don't expect instant results! And don't feel discouraged if your children are older and you feel you haven't taught them enough about order. It's never too late to learn—for you or for your child.

Listed below are some things to keep in mind as you are on the road to organized kids!

- Be consistent! Follow through on any organizational changes, and get your children into the habit of picking up after themselves.
- Make time to get organized. Schedule the time required to implement your plan.
- Doing a *little* is better than doing nothing at all. Set up organizational systems a few at a time.
- During organizing and chore times, maintain a cheerful attitude and encourage your child.
- As soon as they can crawl, teach your children to help with cleaning up.
- Work together with your spouse to teach your child the concept of cooperation.

- Work together as a family. Think of organizational projects the whole family can work on together. Whenever possible, involve your children in family decisions—they'll feel important.
- Show your kids ways they can help other people. This kind of outreach will teach children to think of others instead of focusing only on themselves.
- Don't rob your kids of feeling successful by constantly doing for them the things they can do for themselves.
- Make jobs manageable for your child.
- Remember that when life has order, we have more time to focus on God, on our family, and on ourselves.
- In everything we do, we train our children. They *will* model after us.

I have a wooden heart-shaped sign in my kitchen that my friend Liz gave me. It reads "Ask not what your Mother can do for you, but ask what you can do for your Mother." Pretty good, huh? I believe most kids these days don't help their parents enough. Any time we can allow them to feel responsible, we should. *It helps them!*

CHAPTER 2

Getting Started: Tips and Tools

THE BEST TIP I can give you to help you and your child get organized is to *create a place for everything your child owns*. If you want kids to put things away, *you* have to provide the place. When all your children's things have a designated "home," it will be much easier for them to find stuff and much easier to put stuff away.

How would you feel if you could find anything in your child's room? How would your child feel if he could always find his favorite toy immediately? Almost without exception, I have seen families gain a reassuring sense of control by having their things in order. As everyone goes through their daily routines, they feel far less frenzied and frustrated when the old unorganized chaos is replaced with workable organization techniques.

Kids like structure, and it is a very positive element in our children's lives for two important reasons: (1) it provides a calming sense of security, and (2) it teaches them useful skills for managing their own lives.

For inspiration, take a look at your child's schoolroom. Everything has its place. The teacher has set up specific places for coats and sweaters, books, pencils, chalk, writing paper, and on and on. Teachers will tell you that the students take pride in knowing where everything is kept and want to keep things in their proper place. If one child slips up and puts something on the wrong shelf, another child will quickly point out the mistake.

Teachers know how important it is to have an organized classroom. We moms need to follow this example with our kids' things at home.

At this point you are probably thinking, "If organizing is so easy, then why do I feel so disorganized?" My goal is to help take away your frustration and give you some great tips on simple ways to get your child's stuff organized. I will also recommend useful tools to help keep everything in place. You can do this!

TIPS

Talk with Your Kids

Children love having one-on-one conversations with their parents. We hear it all the time—kids would much rather have time with us than get things from us. As you start the process of getting organized, talk to your children about the ideas you have. Ask for their input too. It's amazing how children have a way of teaching us adults.

Explain to your child that you are going to set up a new organizing system and why you are going to do it. When I organize for Cameron and Collin, I always explain why I am changing things. Once they understand the benefits, they usually accept the new idea with enthusiasm. I get excited about the project and they catch the excitement too. Be positive and have fun when you organize—a good attitude is contagious!

Set an Example

Children follow by example. This truism is a mixed blessing! We love for our children to mimic the good in us, but it hurts when we see them pick up our negative traits. More than likely, if you are disorganized, your child is disorganized as well. It's unfair to get aggravated with our little ones when they are just copying what they have observed in us. Now that you have resolved to bring order to your kids' stuff, everyone will need to adjust to the new plan.

After you put a new organizing system into place, be sure to set the example for keeping things in their new home. It's especially important to follow through in the first few weeks to help everyone establish new patterns. Changing lifelong habits is never easy, but the results will be worth the effort!

With encouragement and consistent consequences, your child will quickly learn to keep her things in order. Even a very young child can put her dirty clothes in the laundry basket, hang her jacket on a hook, and return videotapes to their assigned place. When she is a little older, she can help you keep order by clearing the dinner table and putting clean clothes in their proper place. Children accept these kinds of responsibilities at school without question, and they will accept (and enjoy) them at home as well.

Prepare the Night Before Busy Mornings

Crazy mornings don't benefit anyone, and I can say that with plenty of experience! There have been many mornings that my last words to my boys before getting them on the school bus, were "hurry up!" Mornings go so much more smoothly when my kids and I have prepared ourselves the night before. Whether it's having them pick out their school clothes or making their lunches the night before, your kids will appreciate anything that helps make mornings less hectic.

Use a Color System for More Than One Child

If you have more than one child, the color system is a great way to separate their things. Assign each child his own color (pick their favorite) so that each can always identify his own belongings. For example, let's say you have three kids who share a bathroom. Pick three colors—maybe red, blue, and yellow—and assign a color to each child. Then use that color for each child's towel, toothbrush, comb/brush, bathroom cup, and bathrobe. Your child will always know which item is his, and you'll know who left their towel on the floor! This system also helps prevent the spread of germs when one child is sick.

The color theme can be carried out in other areas of the house as well. For instance, use a child's color for a shoe container in the mudroom or her hamper in the laundry room. If you have a "blankie basket" (a large wicker basket for snuggly throw blankets), have a blanket in each child's color. Children love having their own special things, and having their own special color can really help minimize sibling squabbles.

When your children have toys that are exact duplicates, always label each toy with some kind of distinctive mark so that they can differentiate. Use a permanent marker to write a name, initial, or other symbol so there's never any question about ownership. You might use just a dot in a particular child's special color, particularly on small toys.

Make life easier by labeling your kids' toys with their names.

Purchase Toy-Specific Storage Holders

Toy manufacturers sometimes make special storage boxes that are ideal for a particular toy. These boxes are designed to accommodate a specific toy and its accessories and usually provide compartments to keep all the parts and pieces securely in place.

For example, Collin has a decorated G.I. Joe box that he loves. It's easy to spot, and he always knows exactly what's in that container. Similar kinds of boxes are available for Barbie, Hot Wheels, collector cards, and others. One word of caution, though—before you purchase such a container, look it over carefully to determine whether or not it will work well for you. Sometimes your child's collection might be too large for the container, and occasionally I have seen special containers that are not sturdy enough for long-term use. As a rule, however, they work extremely well. Look for these boxes any time of the year, but especially at Christmas time, when toy companies are geared up for holiday sales.

Give Organizing Gifts to Your Child

With some imagination and little cost, you can choose gifts that will do double duty later as storage containers. For example, at Easter, instead of purchasing an overpriced wicker basket, choose a colorful plastic basket or bin that can be used as a bath caddy or for storing toys. For a great girl's gift, purchase a small lidded box and fill it with hair bows or barrettes.

When you buy a pack of new school pencils, include a useful pencil holder as well. If my sons start collecting a new kind of action figure, I purchase a clear plastic shoe container for their collection and use a paint pen to label the box for the type of toys inside. Kids love to have special places for their special things.

Measure Before Shopping

Save yourself a lot of aggravation by measuring the areas you're organizing. For example, when you plan to buy containers to store on a shelf, measure the length and depth of each shelf. Then you will know what size containers will fit properly on each shelf.

Make Wise Choices for Kids' Furniture

When choosing furniture for your child's room, pick sturdy pieces that will really stand up to hard treatment—nothing spindly or delicate. Look for maximum storage potential in every piece so that you can accommodate all the stuff kids inevitably accumulate.

- Shelving units are my first choice for kids because they offer so much flexibility. Shelves can be used to store almost all toys and all clothing except for hanging items.
- Beds with drawers underneath turn wasted under-the-bed space into useful storage.
- An ideal child's dresser would be one with two to three smaller drawers on top (to separate underwear socks, and other small items) and four large, deep drawers on the bottom. Don't buy a dresser that has only small, shallow drawers—it won't provide enough space and the drawers will end up overstuffed.
- A desk is always functional in a child's room for art projects, homework, and related storage.
- An armoire is a good choice for flexible storage, especially where space is limited.

Organize Kids' Stuff Throughout the House

I'm not suggesting you should allow your child to put his stuff anywhere he wants, but there are some clever ways to hide toys in rooms where you might want a child's play area. For example, my friend Sallie works out of her home, and her son likes to be near her while she works. I helped her set up an area for Tyler in the corner of her office. He keeps some books and art supplies there and "works" alongside Mom.

In my living room, I have a painted bench with a hinged seat that lifts to hide stray toys. When the bench starts to get too full, the boys and I empty it and return the toys to their designated homes.

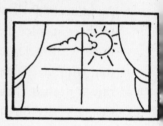

If it is easier for your children to use a downstairs powder room, store a second set of their necessities in an inconspicuous place. If there's no drawer available, a covered wicker basket placed on the floor next to the sink works great for toothbrushes, toothpaste, hairbrushes, and spray water bottles. Having these items readily available on the main floor really helps when you're running late in the morning!

Find unique ways to organize kids' stuff in living areas throughout the house.

Chapter 6, on kitchens, gives some great suggestions on places to put kids' stuff in the kitchen area.

TOOLS

Trash Bags

Clear the room of the trash. I am as sentimental as they come, and I believe there are things we need to keep. But I have also seen so much junk collected in children's rooms that it's impossible to walk without stepping over the litter. Big black trash bags are crucial for clearing out junk. Have plenty on hand.

The next thing to do is pack up outgrown toys and clothes. If your kids are over age five, they might be able to do this part themselves. A trick I've shared with clients is to pay your child a certain sum of money to make a really big pile of stuff to give away. Tell them they can buy that Nintendo game or something else they really want! Donate toys, clothes, and other items no longer used to a local charity for a tax deduction.

Containers

There are many tools you can use to get organized, but if I had to pick the most beneficial tool, it would have to be containers. Containers come in a variety of sizes, and they are absolutely the best option for sorting and separating things. You can't have too many containers. Listed

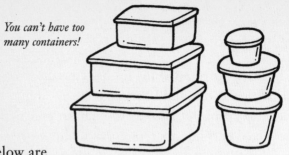

You can't have too many containers!

below are container suggestions and examples of uses:

Rubbermaid (or something comparable) clear containers: These containers are probably the most valuable of all. There are endless uses for clear containers. They stack great, and you can see what's inside. Get them in a variety of sizes, from shoebox size to the large flat ones that can slide under the bed. Buy them whenever you see them on sale and store them for future use. When a need arises for a container, you'll have one on hand.

Rubbermaid colored containers: I love the Rubbermaid Roughneck 18-gallon size. I buy them in colors that represent what I am storing inside. I have them stacked in the garage for all my holiday stuff. For Christmas, I use red; for summer stuff, blue (the color of water); for Thanksgiving things, I found a rust-colored one (the color of fall leaves). I label all my containers in large letters with a thick black permanent marker on at least two sides.

This is also a great size for storing a large bag of dog food. Put a big scoop inside, and give your child the chore of feeding the dog. The tight seal keeps the food fresh and also helps keep bugs out.

Extra-large Rubbermaid containers: I'm talking about the really big 50-plus gallon containers. I love these for the garage and basement. They are great for storing all kinds of camping stuff and other large items. (If you ever have a flood in your basement, you will be really glad you used these containers!)

Another terrific idea for these containers is to use them for storing extra blankets. My sons love to make "tents" and big blanket "beds" on the floor. But when they're finished playing, the job of folding all the blankets and returning them to the shelves is a time-consuming chore. So I bought the biggest Rubbermaid container I could find, and now that's where we keep all the blankets. Now, after the boys are through playing, they just stuff the blankets back in the container. No more folding! Every month or so, I wash all the blankets to keep them clean and fresh.

Wicker baskets: I will admit that one of my nicknames has been "basket queen." I love wicker baskets—they are decorative, useful, and look good in every room in the house. Because most wicker baskets have handles, they are great for toddlers to use when carrying their special stuff. Whenever I go to my kids' classrooms for parties or just to help out, I use a large wicker basket to carry my goodies.

Plastic baskets: These come in a variety of sizes and colors and can be used for holding all sorts of things. I like that I can put smaller plastic baskets in the dishwasher to get cleaned.

Wicker baskets are decorative and useful.

Pails/Buckets: Big buckets are ideal for use in the garage to store old tennis balls or to "stand up" plastic bats. Each of my boys has his own fun-colored, lime green pail to catch frogs or whatever!

Trash cans with lids: The aluminum trash can is perfect to use for potting soil. Let your little ones grab buckets of dirt to help you in the garden.

Bins: Stack them in the mudroom, garage, closets, pantry, etc. Bins can hold all sorts of things. Keep one for shoes in the mudroom or bath toys in the bathroom.

Toy boxes: I'm not a big fan of throwing all kinds of toys into a toy box. Everything inside usually turns into a big mess. If you have a toy box, use it for certain collections only, such as stuffed animals or balls. Toy boxes that have a hinged cover (that closes safely and slowly) are great because they hide the contents as well as provide a place to sit.

Dressers: If you have an extra dresser other than the one your child uses for his clothes, store it in a closet and use the drawers as containers. Dresser drawers are great for storing puzzles, Barbies, and other groups of toys. Remember to give each drawer a purpose—don't use them as catchalls!

Under-the-bed drawers: My son Collin has two drawers under his bed. We use them to store all his cars and trucks. He can sit on the floor, open his drawer, and play. When he is finished, he puts his cars away and closes the drawer.

Stackable plastic drawers: I love these inexpensive drawers and recommend them to all my clients. They are easy for kids to open, come in a variety of sizes, and are great for taking advantage of the otherwise wasted floor space inside closets. Collin doesn't have a dresser, and we use stackable drawers for his clothes.

Another idea for stackable drawers is for gift-wrapping supplies. I made one for my friend Sallie, to organize all her wrapping paper, bows, ribbon, cards, and gifts. I labeled each drawer with its contents, and she now has an easy time finding all the things she needs to wrap the perfect gift. Also, by using her gift-wrapping area, Sallie is teaching her kids about the importance of doing special things for others.

Plastic drawer dividers: These dividers are terrific for organizing and separating things inside your drawers. They can be found in your local discount store displayed with plastic kitchen organizers.

Stackable plastic drawers ar great for taking up wasted closet floor space.

Cardboard shoe-boxes: Use them to divide socks, underwear, tights, and other small items in your child's dresser. Boot boxes will work better for bulkier items.

Jars: Glass or clear plastic jars are great for separating and storing craft supplies.

Tupperware: Since the lids are so secure, Tupperware is a good container for storing things that have a lot of little pieces.

Plastic wash basins: You probably received one of these basins when you brought your baby home from the hospital. You can also find them in discount stores at very little cost. They are great to hold things that don't need a top. Decorate with paint pens or stickers to make them more fun.

Lockers: There are two kinds of lockers: the ones we see in school hallways and the ones we used for packing our college stuff. My son Cameron has both kinds. The taller one is very cool-looking in his sports-themed room, but really isn't as efficient as I would like. We keep it because he likes to keep special stuff in there. I do like the other kind because it can store all sorts of things from keepsakes to G.I. Joes (what Cameron has in his).

Zip-lock bags: Whoever invented zip-lock bags deserves a big kiss from every mom. Use them to separate stuff inside containers.

Stackable letter trays: Organize your child's desk as efficiently as you would organize your own. Stackable trays are great for organizing notebook paper, construction paper, art paper, and things of this size.

Picture boxes: These inexpensive cardboard boxes designed to store snapshots and negatives make excellent organizers. They are available in a variety of designs so that you can choose one to match your décor. I talk more about these boxes in Chapter 10, "Organizing Keepsakes."

Tool, tackle, or makeup boxes: These boxes are already set up with different compartments built-in. They usually have a handle, so they are easy to carry. Use them for crafts, doll accessories, micro-machines, hobbies, and, of course, for what they were originally intended.

Screw/Nail compartmentalized boxes: I love these boxes for storing craft beads.

Mugs or vases: Great for storing pencils, markers, pens, and similar supplies.

Baby wipe containers: These sturdy flip-top boxes can be used to store crayons, stickers, barrettes, small jars of paint, or other small items.

Shelves

Every child should have some sort of shelving unit in his or her room. Refer to Chapter 3 for shelving ideas.

Hooks

I love hooks! Hooks make it so easy for kids to hang stuff, and there are lots of fun decorative hooks available. Hang simple, rounded hooks on the back of bedroom, bathroom, and closet doors. When you position hooks for children to use, make sure they are low enough for little ones to reach.

E Z Anchors

These anchors used to hang shelves or hooks are the greatest! Don't get any other brand; they don't work as well. Home Depot (in the hardware section) is the only place I know to get them. They are very easy to install, and each anchor holds up to fifty pounds.

Cardboard Filing Boxes

You can usually find these boxes in sets of three in discount and office supply stores. I use them for storing my kids' school papers. I also use them to store "to grow into" clothes, which I talk about in detail in Chapter 5, "Nursery and Baby Items."

Permanent Markers or Paint Pens

Label everything! Purchase a variety of permanent markers and paint pens and stash them somewhere safe from little hands. Label all containers and boxes so you don't have to open each one to find out what's inside.

WHERE TO FIND ORGANIZATIONAL TOOLS

The first place to look for organizational tools such as the ones mentioned above is to go through your house, attic, or basement. Garage sales will also produce some great finds. Mostly, however, I purchase my organizing stuff at local discount department stores. I love specialty stores, such as The Container Store, but have found many items to be overpriced compared with similar items in discount department stores.

CHAPTER 3

Bedrooms, closets, Dressers, and Desks

BRINGING ORDER INTO YOUR child's bedroom brings many benefits to both you and your child! First, order *reduces daily stress*. An organized room eliminates the frustration that results when your children can't find the things they need. Second, order *encourages appreciation*. When your children can clearly see everything they have, they gain an appreciation for all they are blessed with. Third, order *teaches responsibility*. When you set up systems and routines in your children's rooms, they learn to be responsible for following the rules of order. And fourth, order *reflects love*. One of the best reasons to organize your children's bedrooms is to make them feel special and important.

I say it over and over, but I believe with all my heart that when you make special places for your children's things, it makes them feel special. My boys *love* having neat and organized rooms, and whenever I make improvements or add something new, they know I am doing something special just for them.

One of the best reasons to organize your child's bedroom is to make him feel special and important.

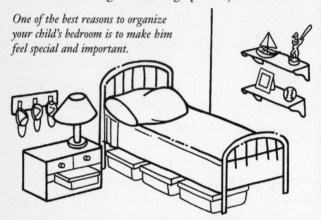

Initially, it does take some time and creativity as well as a little expense, but the payoff makes it all worthwhile! When you create bedrooms that kids feel good about, they are far more likely to take care of their stuff! And, when you designate a place for everything in their rooms, your kids won't get so frustrated when you ask them to clean up. Have you helped your child set up a functional and fun bedroom? Does your child love his room? If his room, closet, and dresser drawers could use some help, here are some simple ideas for you that really work.

BEDROOMS

Get the Trash Bags Ready

If your child's room is a real mess, this first step will not be fun. Unfortunately, it's a job that has to be done. Before you can organize any room, you must get rid of all the unnecessary stuff. It is much better to begin this project when your child is not present—children never want to get rid of anything, even if they have forgotten about its existence.

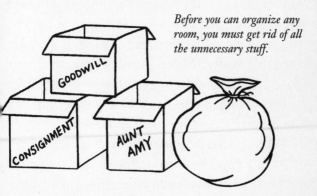

Before you can organize any room, you must get rid of all the unnecessary stuff.

Be careful not to throw away anything that is important to your child. The goal of organizing is to bring peace, and hurting your child's feelings will not accomplish the goal. As your child's parent, you know what's important to him. If you're not sure about something, you may want to put the item aside until you can talk with your child about it.

With that in mind, the first thing you need to do is bring in a large garbage bag for trash and also a few large boxes for outgrown items that are still in good condition. Be sure to label each box with a marker designating "Goodwill," "consignment shop," or the name of a friend who has younger children.

Gather up all trash and put it into the trash bag. Next, remove everything that is no longer used by your child. Place the outgrown clothing and toys into their assigned boxes. Broken toys that can't be easily repaired will go into the trash bag. If there are items that really belong in other rooms of your house, take them out. I suggest that you start under the bed, and then take one area at a time until you have covered the entire room and closet.

When you are through discarding, stand back and take a good look around to decide if there is any furniture that should be removed. Furniture for kids should be sturdy and functional—a kid's room is not the place for a wobbly table or an antique lamp. If there is anything that doesn't qualify or doesn't serve a real need, remove it and find another place for it.

Now that you have gotten rid of everything your child no longer needs, give the room a good cleaning.

Personalize Your Child's Room

Before we start talking about ideas to organize the space, we need to think about how to make your child's room feel special to her. By personalizing your child's room, you help her develop a sense of her own self-worth. A child who feels good about her room is more likely to appreciate it and take care of it.

By personalizing your child's room, you help her develop her own sense of self-worth.

As a single parent, I live on a strict budget. I can't spend a lot of money on decorating, yet both of my boys love their rooms because I have found creative ways to fit their rooms to their individual personalities.

Collin loves the color red, so I use a lot of red in his room. I purchased inexpensive old picture frames at garage sales, sanded them down a little, and painted them red. Then I put photos in them that I knew would make him smile. I recycled his old

red crib sheet as a cover for an oversized bed pillow. After I made the simple cover, I bought some
white iron-on fabric letters and spelled out his name
on one side of the pillow. He loves it! Around his
white wooden mirror frame I wrote with a red paint
pen "Collin is very special." His room is his own personal space.

Cameron loves sports. Each wall in his room is
decorated with a different sports theme. One wall
has baseball stuff, one has football stuff, and another one has basketball stuff. Every accessory I have
purchased for his room has a sports theme. For
example, he has a Sammy Sosa wastebasket next to
his baseball wall. He has a Dallas Cowboys lamp
near the football wall. His friends love his room!
Sometimes I think his walls look a little junky with
all the posters, but *he* really likes it, and that's what's
important.

Cameron also collects baseball hats. It was a real
challenge trying to figure out how to hang all his
hats so he could pick and choose from them daily. At
Home Depot, I bought a long piece of finished
wood. I hammered in nails about a hat width apart
and then hung it on the wall for his hats. It worked,
and he loved it!

Cameron is also my artist. From the time he was
old enough to draw, he has had art materials on his

desk. With creative tools always handy, Cameron has become a terrific artist. Many of his masterpieces are hanging throughout our home!

Think about the things you can do to personalize your child's room. Is he fascinated with dinosaurs? Does she love playing with her dolls? Maybe your child has a collection of toy cars or stuffed animals that could be organized and displayed. Your child is unique, and the personal touches you add to his room will make him feel that he is special.

When Your Kids Share a Room

Everybody needs a spot to call his own, and it is especially important to create personal space when children share a bedroom. You can make special places for each child even in a small, crowded room.

If your children share a bedroom, make sure they have their own special places within the room.

Pretend there is an imaginary line down the center of the room and give each child half of the room.

You can even use furniture to divide the room. For example, if you are using twin beds, let each child have his own space in the area around each bed. Give each child his own bookshelf or a special chair to put on his side of the room. If you have a boy and a girl sharing a room, each can have his or her preference of toys in their space. Having his own defined space will also help your child feel more secure when friends come to visit because it will be obvious whose toys are whose.

A bedside table between the beds could be the dividing line down the room. Each child could have an equal amount of drawer space in the bedside table and share the items on top such as a lamp, telephone, and clock.

If your children share a fairly large room, you might place two freestanding bookshelves back to back in the center of the room. Each child's bookcase would face his or her side of the room, thereby creating two distinct areas. Use your imagination and be creative—your kids will love it!

If your budget allows, you might consider a built-in half wall to use as a room divider. You can get a similar effect by using purchased room dividers such as decorative screens or the kind of dividers used for office cubicles.

One positive thing about giving each child his own space is that he will also have the responsibility of only that part of the room. Then you know which one is the culprit if there is clutter! Explain to the children that each is individually responsible for cleaning and keeping his or her own part of the room neat and organized.

Set up Shelving Units

Remember that the key to organization is finding places to put stuff. Shelves are great for organizing kids' things, and they can also be used to display your child's special things.

If you don't already have shelves in your child's room, look around the house or basement for anything that will work for you. You can also check garage sales for inexpensive shelving units. If you find something sturdy that is the right size but looks somewhat shabby, consider how it would look with a fresh coat of paint.

Another shelf source is hardware and discount stores. They sell laminated pre-measured shelves that are easy to install. Or, if you are handy, you can make a simple shelf unit. The point is to get some sort of shelves for your child's room. Shelves help keep things off the floor!

If your children are sharing a room, have a shelving unit for each child because every child has his own special stuff to display.

When organizing shelving units, give each shelf a purpose. For example, one shelf might be for books (put books on the bottom shelf for toddlers), another shelf for awards and trophies. I like to use the very top shelf for things like keepsakes, baby albums, and heirlooms. If your child knows each shelf is for something special, he will be less likely to put a bunch of junk there!

My son Collin loves his toy collections. He collects such things as animals, bugs, army men, and *Lion King* characters. I grouped each collection in a clear plastic box and stacked them on two of his shelves. He loves having his collections all together!

When organizing shelving units, give each shelf a purpose.

When you create containers for your kids, label each one with either words or a picture to show what's inside. Paint pens, permanent markers, and stickers work great. Then they'll know exactly where to find certain toys and exactly where to put them away!

Make a "Blue Box"

I received a blue plastic wash basin when I was in the hospital giving birth to my first son, Cameron. I've always been pretty creative utilizing all sorts of containers and decided to make this container "Cameron's blue box."

I decorated the box by writing his name all over the outside. As all children do, Cameron started collecting special little "stuff," and I trained him to put all his special stuff in his blue box. When he would ask me, "Mom, have you seen my rock?" I would say, "Did you look in your blue box?" Both my boys still put their special stuff in their blue boxes. This is a great place for birthday party favors and all the little bitty stuff you don't know where else to put. Of course, the box doesn't have to be blue. If your little girl likes the color pink, get her a pink box.

Utilize Under-the-Bed Storage

Under-the-bed storage containers are wonderful for storing all sorts of things. They also help prevent stuff from being thrown under the bed since something is already occupying the space! Plastic containers cost a little more than cardboard ones, but I think plastic is worth the additional expense. Cardboard boxes are not as sturdy and don't protect the contents against moisture as well as plastic ones do.

Your child's artwork, sports clothing, out-of-season clothes, Lego pieces (it's easy to see the pieces when they are spread over a large area), Barbie dolls, puzzles, scrapbooks, picture albums, and keepsakes are all items that work great in under-the-bed containers.

When toys are stored in under-the-bed containers, the containers can easily be pulled out for play and pushed back under when it's clean-up time!

Keep Things Off the Floor

We have already talked about freestanding shelving units as a great way to keep things off the floor. Another shelving idea is to install high shelves as a decorative effect near the ceiling. These shelves can hold toys, trophies, collectibles, dolls, stuffed animals, and other items you want to display but don't want your child to play with.

Another terrific idea is to install hooks on walls. I love hooks and have them everywhere in my house. Hooks make it easy to hang stuff up. You can use all sorts of hooks—individual hooks, hook bars, decorative hooks—for such things as hats, robes, jackets, towels, and baseball gloves.

gh shelves are orative and functional.

Purchase a freestanding coatrack. I recommend one that is sturdy and will not topple over easily. My friend Sue has one for her son, Brandon. His coatrack holds all his Boy Scout stuff, so that when he's getting ready for a scout meeting, he knows where everything is. Coatracks are also great places to hang not-quite-dirty clothes to air out before hanging them back in the closet.

Solutions for Stuffed Animals

What child doesn't have at least five stuffed animals? I recommended using shelves earlier, and this is an especially good idea if your child has a lot of stuffed animals. I have also used large round plastic containers or a toy box for stuffed animals. I tell them that this is for *stuffed animals only* so it makes it easy for them to find a particular animal they may want to play with. I also have a separate large wicker basket for Collin's smaller bean-stuffed animals.

You can also purchase nets to hold stuffed animals. I have actually attached one of these nets to the foot end of the top bunk bed. It was a great place to store the animals off the floor and easy for the kids to reach.

Create a Reading Corner

When I organize children's rooms, one of my favorite things to create is a cozy reading corner. Having a special place to sit (a child-sized chair, couch, or bean bag, or a pile of oversized pillows), ample lighting, and lots of age-appropriate books, gives a child the perfect reading area. Use a small shelving unit to house the books.

In providing your child with a special place to read, you encourage him to spend some quiet time reading on his own. Donate books your child no longer reads to a local charity, shelter, or hospital.

Encourage reading by making a special reading corner for your child.

Take a Picture of Their Clean Room

This idea may sound silly, but when she has a picture of her orderly room, your child has no excuse for saying, "I don't know where everything goes!"

CLOSETS

Hang Things on Hangers

A closet looks so much neater when the hangers are all the same size and color. Purchasing hangers in your child's favorite color is an additional expense, but I think it's worth it. The added touch will make his or her closet more special. Check the Sunday paper for sales on hangers. For kids age five and under, buy the smaller, kid-sized hangers.

Your child will appreciate a well-organized closet.

Group Like Clothes Together

When organizing your child's clothes, hang all of the same types of clothes together. This system makes it easy for your child to find

what he's looking for. For example, hang all pants together, all dresses together, all short sleeve shirts together. If you have an extra closet in another room, store out-of-season clothes there. By doing this, you allow more space in your child's bedroom closet.

Use Plastic Containers

When you use containers, the clothes don't get thrown all over the closet. Clear plastic containers with lids are great to place on closet shelves to hold all sorts of miscellaneous items. For example, use a container to store winter gear such as gloves, hats, scarves, and thermal underwear. Or use one to store gymnastic clothing, keepsakes, baby clothes, and out-of-season clothes.

Organize "Giveaway" Clothes

Kids grow too quickly! Establishing a system to remove clothes that no longer fit will help to keep your child's closet orderly.

I recommend having at least one box placed in the closet for you and your child to put clothes that she will no longer wear. Call it the giveaway box. In this box would be clothes that will be thrown away, donated to a charity, consigned, sold in a garage sale, or given to relatives or friends. You can take it even further and make a box for each purpose; it all depends on what you intend to do with the clothes. I like to use new, clean, plain boxes. To avoid confusion, label each box clearly.

Organize "To Grow Into" Clothes

I talk about this in detail in Chapter 5, "Nursery and Baby Items." Use this same principle with your older children.

Organize "Keepsake" Clothes

I discuss organizing keepsakes in Chapter 5, "Nursery and Baby Items," as well as in Chapter 10, "Keepsakes."

Buy a Back-of-the-Door Shoe Hanger

I love these hangers. Purchase the kind with plastic kid-sized pockets. They are handy to store not only shoes but also other kid items such as rolled belts, hair bows, socks, Beanie Babies, gloves, and other small items.

Install a Lower Shelf in Your Child's Closet

Installing a shelf below your child's hanging clothes works great to store bulky jeans, sweaters, and sweat pants and shirts. Most often the only shelf installed in kids' closets is too high for them to reach.

When you install a lower shelf, your child can reach his or her own clothes (and put them away as well!). This shelf should be installed under clothes that do not hang very long, such as blouses, shirts, and folded pants. You can also line this shelf with plastic containers for all sorts of things such as toys, hobbies, underwear, and dance clothes.

Organizing the Closet Floor

The best way to prevent the closet floor from becoming a big junk pile is to organize it with storage containers. My favorite kind of storage container to use on a closet floor is plastic stackable drawers, available in a variety of sizes. The really big ones are the best! I have also mentioned storing an extra dresser in your child's closet to take up space and prevent clutter. This approach also gives you extra drawers with which to work. Have a purpose for the containers you store in your child's closet. And remember, the fewer places to throw stuff, the less stuff thrown!

Purchase a Laundry Basket for Your Child's Closet

Put a laundry basket in each child's closet for dirty clothes. If your children are physically able to carry it, let them bring the basket to the laundry room when it is time to wash their things. In the laundry room, have them empty their laundry baskets into two different laundry baskets—one for whites and one for colored clothes. Teach them how to separate their clothes and explain why it's necessary. In my laundry room, I use a white basket for white clothes and a blue one for colored clothes. Color coding makes it easy for my sons to know which clothes go into which basket.

To make life easier, one of my clients has three tall white hampers with lids in her laundry room. In black permanent marker she has written *white*, *light*, and *dark* on her hampers. Her dirty clothes are already sorted when she begins to do the wash!

DRESSERS

Empty Every Drawer

I'm sure my clients hate it when I do this, but it has to be done! The only way to clean out drawers is to empty them completely. Remove all the clothes that no longer fit or are no longer worn and put them in the trash or in your giveaway box. Clean out all candy wrappers and miscellaneous trash. Now you are ready to start organizing your child's dresser.

Make Each Drawer Have a Purpose

Set up a system for your children's drawers, *explaining clearly to them what you are doing*. For example, tell them that the top left drawer is for socks only. The top right drawer is for underwear only. The middle left drawer is for pajamas only. The middle right drawer is for T-shirts only. Understanding the system will make it easier for your child to find stuff and put stuff away.

Paint Pictures on Drawers or Knobs

Make it easy for little ones who can't read by having a picture of the drawer's contents on the outside of the drawer or on the knob. I have actually seen knobs sold like this. Or paint a picture yourself. You don't have to be an artist; just a simple drawing will do. You can also decoupage a picture of the appropriate item onto the drawer or knob.

Make organizing easy for your little ones.

Use Drawer Dividers

If your child's dresser has only large drawers, use drawer dividers for the little stuff such as socks or underwear. Cardboard shoeboxes work great. Boot size boxes might work even better, depending on drawer size. Of course, you can always use plastic containers or any other kind of container or box to separate stuff in the drawer.

Make a Game Out of It

All kids love games and challenges, so make it a game to see who can straighten his drawers the fastest. It works like a charm with my boys!

I start with "on your mark, get set, go" and encourage them along the way, giving them a certain amount of time to accomplish the task. The challenge is to see who can organize his drawers the fastest. I let each child feel like a winner by complimenting who finished first, who had the neatest T-shirt drawer, etc. Then I do something special for each child after he has finished. Organizing can be fun!

Top of Dresser

One thing you want to try to do is keep the top of the dresser from becoming a dumping ground. If you arrange the top of the dresser in a special way for your child, she will be less likely to junk it up. And if it is special enough, she'll want to keep it that way. Less is definitely better when arranging the top of your child's dresser.

If you have an infant and need a changing table, you might consider using the top of the dresser for this purpose. I used this idea for Collin when he was a baby, and it worked really well. Refer to Chapter 5 for more on this subject.

Recycle Old Dressers

If you have a dresser you are considering throwing away, use the drawers for under-the-bed storage containers.

ENCOURAGE WORK HABITS WITH A DESK

I believe every child should have a desk. When children have their very own desk, they feel grownup and important. Desks encourage good work and study habits, and provide a perfect place for creative projects. You don't need to buy anything elaborate—a card table and chair can work as a desk! Just make a special place for your children to do their "work."

Organize Their Desks with Supplies

Kids love to have their very own office supplies. Remember the section about giving organizational gifts to children? Desk supplies make great gifts.

Provide your child with her own tape dispenser (the heavy kind from an office supply store), stapler, ruler, scissors, pencils (with her name on them!), colored pencils, electric pencil sharpener, pens,

dren love to their own and office lies.

markers, notebook paper, construction paper, stationery, thank you notes, and dictionary. Use baskets, jars, stackable letter trays, and drawer dividers to organize everything and encourage neatness.

Purchase a desk lamp to provide adequate lighting. As a finishing touch, hang a bulletin board above your child's desk to hang a calendar, special notes, awards, pictures, and cards.

CHAPTER 4

Bathrooms

THE BATHROOM MAY BE the smallest room in the house, but kids usually make the biggest mess there. This is an important room to organize for your children because it is where they learn to keep themselves groomed and clean. If the necessary tools and supplies are readily accessible, your children will be more independent with bathroom duties. We also know that this is a place where your children will be "still" for a while, and I'll give you some great ideas for them to utilize that time!

Remember, as with any room, if the bathroom has special places for kids' personal stuff, they will more likely keep their things organized.

USE HOOKS

I have found that kids have a hard time hanging towels neatly on towel bars, so I've replaced the towel bars in my kids' bathroom with some sort of hook. Hooks make it easy for kids to hang and remove towels, bathing suits, and damp clothing. There are many types of hooks available, but the cheapest and most efficient are wooden boards that have wooden pegs attached. They are widely available at many stores including Lowe's and Michael's. Usually, these boards have at least three pegs, but the more the better, especially when several children share a bathroom. If you like, you can paint them to match your bathroom décor.

You can also find fun individual hooks to hang in the bathroom. Place one next to the tub for easy access to a bath towel, and hang one next to the sink for a hand towel. I've been told that I get a little hook crazy, but I like to make life easy for myself, my kids, and my guests. I install hooks on the back of every bathroom door as well as on bedroom and closet doors. (For safety, use rounded hooks in kids' areas.) Since my two boys share a bathroom, I have two hooks on the back of their bathroom door for their bathrobes. The hook for my younger son, Collin, is installed much lower than the one for

Cameron. I always try to put myself in their shoes (or slippers!) and allow them to be independent whenever possible. To make it extra special, use a paint pen to write each child's name over his own hook.

Hooks make it easy for kids to hang things up.

BEGIN WITH BATH TOYS

Kids love to play with toys in the tub, and there are several ways to keep tub toys organized. I like plastic baskets with holes in the sides so you can shake the basket to get out any accumulated water. A small laundry basket will work for this purpose if you have a lot of tub toys to store. If you want the tub toys out of sight, you can store them in a plastic basket under the sink. Or, if you have a towel closet in the kids' bathroom, you can store the plastic basket on a shelf or on the floor.

If you have a kid-friendly bathroom and don't mind toys in sight, you can store them in "toy nets" that attach to the walls with suction cups. However, your bathroom walls must be real ceramic tile so that the suction cups will adhere well. Some of my friends love these nets, but I find it sometimes difficult to get the toys in and out of them. For my boys, I use a tub rack that lies across the tub. These racks, available in plastic or metal, are designed to hold bath necessities, but my kids use theirs as a play station for their action figures.

Remember to disinfect bath toys and storage tubs every couple of weeks to kill any mildew or germs. Simply fill the tub with water, add a cup of chlorine bleach, and let the toys soak for a minute or two.

KEEP COUNTERTOPS FREE FROM CLUTTER

Keep countertops as free of clutter as possible. Not only will the room look neater, cleaning will be a lot easier if you don't have to shift a lot of stuff. If you are lucky enough to have drawers in your kids' bathroom, utilize them efficiently to store daily bathroom supplies. If not, here are some suggestions for keeping items on the countertop:

Keep countertops free from clutter.

- Stack inexpensive white washcloths in a basket. White is best because you can use bleach to keep them sanitary.
- Have a toothbrush holder or a special cup for each child to store his own toothbrush.
- Small square tissue boxes require the least amount of counter space. Use a box holder to protect the cardboard box from water splashes.
- Use a plastic basket with handles to store the things your kids use every day (lotion, hair brushes, deodorant, etc.). A basket with handles makes it easy to remove items when cleaning.
- A decorative dispenser filled with liquid antibacterial soap creates less of a mess than bar soap.
- Clear plastic containers with lids keep cotton swabs and cotton balls dust and germ free.

ORGANIZE BATHROOM DRAWERS

If you have bathroom drawers, you can hide some of the items that would otherwise be in sight on the counter. Use plastic drawer dividers to separate items and keep order. You can find plastic dividers in the kitchenwares department of stores like K-Mart, Wal-Mart, or Target. They are ideal

for organizing toothpaste, dental floss, hairbrushes, barrettes, and other items kids use rou-
tinely. These dividers hook onto each other, and
come in a variety of lengths and widths.
Remember, when you are organizing drawers, it
helps to categorize each one. For example, have a
drawer for hair stuff only.

MAKE A CLEANING SUPPLY BASKET AND CLEANING INSTRUCTIONS LIST

Teach and encourage your children from a
young age to help keep the bathroom neat and
clean. Start by filling a plastic tote basket with all
the age-appropriate supplies your child needs to
clean the bathroom properly. Store the basket under
the sink or in a bathroom closet. (Install childproof
safety locks on the cabinet or door if you have
young children who need to be protected from
cleaning compounds.)

The key to a good cleaning is clear instructions.
My friend Suzanne gave me this tip. Make an item-
ized list of everything your kids need to know in
order to clean the bathroom. Many times we
assume our kids know exactly what to do, when
they usually have no idea! Be explicit with your
instructions; cover each detail no matter how
simple it may seem. For example, "Cleaning the

mirror—Spray the entire mirror with glass cleaner, then wipe it dry with paper towels. Try to not leave streaks on the mirror." Or " Cleaning the toilet— Spray the entire toilet with bathroom cleaner. Spray the top, sides, bottom, and both sides of the seat completely and wipe dry with paper towels or clean dry cloth."

If they know exactly what to do, your kids will get great satisfaction from doing a great job!

WHILE THEY ARE "STILL"

Any time I can get my child's full attention, I try to utilize it the best way I can. As they sit and do their business, here are some ideas that will help keep their minds occupied.

Hang a bulletin board close to the toilet. This is a great place to leave special notes for your child, Scripture verses, words of encouragement, or spelling words to learn. Let your kids hang whatever they want there, too. Decorate or paint the board to match your bathroom's décor.

Place a wicker or plastic basket on the floor next to the toilet and fill it with positive reading material. For example, in our basket I put in a book on manners and another book titled *10,000 Things to Be Happy About.* Cameron has told me many times about the things he has read in these books.

KEEP THE BATHROOM WELL-STOCKED WITH SUPPLIES

Keeping the bathroom well-stocked keeps us from hearing *"MOM!"* from little ones who run out of toilet paper. Keep extra rolls of paper within reach of the toilet. If a cabinet is not close enough, fill a wicker basket with toilet paper rolls and place it by the side of the toilet. You can also use a small table near the toilet to hold necessities. A small end table with deep drawers or a cabinet door also work great for this purpose.

When your daughter begins menstruation, keep plenty of personal care supplies handy for her. A rectangular covered wicker basket placed on top of the toilet works great for storing such items.

Stock backup supplies for items such as toothpaste, soap, and shampoo. Keep them all together in a plastic container. Always store the container in the same spot so your child will know where to look when the item runs out.

FILL A FIRST-AID CONTAINER OR DRAWER

Fill a container or drawer with everything you need to fix a cut, scratch, or sting. If you use a container, always store it in the same place so that you don't have to search for it during an emergency.

CHAPTER 5

Nursery and Baby Items

I THINK THE MOST frustrated mother is a new mother. Everything is a new experience, and most new mothers don't really know what to expect. Even new mothers who already have other children can be overwhelmed with a new addition to the family. Whether you are a first-time mom or have several kids, you can simplify your life by learning new ways to organize all that baby stuff. Give the baby a pacifier, pour yourself a cup of tea, and take a few minutes to discover some easy ways to streamline your routine.

THE NURSERY

Babies truly are a gift from God! They are so precious, and they can stir our deepest emotions. I remember times I actually cried from sheer happiness while I nursed my boys in the middle of the night. Then there were other nights when I became totally exasperated because of missed sleep due to baby care! The point is, babies make enormous demands on us, and we need to set up systems to minimize our effort to meet those demands.

There are a few things you can do when setting up your baby's room to make it work more efficiently for you.

- One of your first purchases for a nursery should be a good, comfortable rocking chair. There is no substitute for a rocking chair to soothe a fussy baby, and it's the ideal place to nurse your baby. Place the rocker next to a table of some sort so you can keep a bottle or glass of water nearby. (Nursing moms get thirsty!)
- Keep a clock in view so that you can note how long the baby nursed and at what time.
- Fill a wicker basket with folded cloth diapers and place it on the table. When the baby spits up, you will have the necessary items to clean it up at hand!
- For convenience, set up the changing table near the crib.

- To save steps, place a diaper pail next to the changing table.
- Keep a box of trash bags for the diaper pail close by—either on the changing table or in a dresser drawer.

Install Shelves under Hanging Rod in Closet

Shelves are especially helpful when you don't have a separate dresser for the baby. Line the shelves with plastic baskets or containers. Use shoebox size or larger depending on what is going inside, and use one container for each type of baby item. For example, have a container for socks only, T-shirts only, baby blankets only, and hats only. This will make it easy for you to find exactly what you need without having to sort through piles of baby things. When you install the topmost shelf, be sure to leave enough room to accommodate any clothes you want to hang from the rod.

Hang an Over-the-Door Shoe Holder Inside Closet

Purchase a shoe holder in either plastic or canvas and use it as a catchall for miscellaneous baby stuff such as hair bows, tights, socks, and mittens. And, since it's hanging inside the closet, it's out of sight!

Line Dresser Drawers with Containers

Use plastic or cardboard shoeboxes to organize dresser drawers. The containers will keep small articles of clothing from becoming jumbled together. Then categorize each drawer; for example, designate the top drawer for sleepwear.

Plan a Well-Equipped Changing Area

Your life will be a lot easier if you keep the changing area well-stocked and organized with all the things you need to change a diaper. If your baby is a boy, you have probably already discovered that he will "shower" you with love if you don't put his diaper on fast enough!

For my son Collin, I used a dresser for a changing table. I covered the top with a thick pad and kept his diaper-changing things handy in the top dresser drawer. His clothes were easily accessible from the lower drawers. This plan worked well for us and is a great alternative to a separate changing table.

Be sure to keep tabs on the diaper supply and replenish it well before you run out. Better yet, stock up when you find diapers on sale and store the extras in the closet.

Organize Crib Bedding

Store all crib sheets, pillow covers, sheet protectors, and baby blankets together. If you have installed shelving in your baby's closet, you might choose to keep bed linens on a selected shelf. You might also store the bedding in a dresser drawer or the regular linen closet.

If you are like me, you will agree that changing crib sheets is a hassle! Life is difficult enough, so I like to make things as easy as I can. One thing you can do is select cotton knit sheets instead of standard woven sheets. Since knits stretch, they are easier to pull over the mattress. You can also buy fancy sheet sets that have a top sheet that lies flat over the mattress and attaches with Velcro or elastic strips. These work great but are expensive. You can get a similar benefit by using a terry cloth or cotton sheet protector over the area where your baby's head lies and most stains occur. When it's soiled, you can wash just the protector, not the sheet.

BABY ITEMS

Carry a Well-Stocked, Attractive Diaper Bag

Since you are going to live with it every day for a couple of years, splurge on a well-designed diaper bag you really like. You might want to consider one of the newer, more tailored designs that look more like a handbag than a diaper bag. Whatever your choice, stock it with all the things you need for your baby's emergencies: diapers, wipes, travel size bottles of lotion, medicine, teething cookies, pacifier, bottles (water, juice, formula), formula powder, baby food, thermometer, etc. Check your bag before you leave home, especially if you are going to be away for an extended period of time.

Make Bath Time Easy

Holding a wet baby can be a tricky thing! The key to easy bath time is having all the bathing essentials close at hand. Fill a plastic bath basket with handles with everything you need to give baby a bath: baby shampoo, baby soap, wash cloth, yellow ducky, etc. You can carry it with you to the kitchen if you bathe your baby in the sink or in a baby bathtub, or you can set it on the floor next to your bathroom tub.

Remember to disinfect bath toys and storage tubs every couple of weeks to kill any mildew or germs. Simply fill the tub with water, add a cup of chlorine bleach, and let the toys soak for a minute or two. Then rinse.

Create a Baby Basket

My girlfriend Liz gave me this great tip. Purchase a large, attractive wicker basket or use one that you already have. Fill it with all the things you need for routine baby care: diapers, diaper pins, wipes, ointment, lotion, brush and comb, infant nail

y basket will help simplify
r a new mother.

clippers, pacifier, baby Tylenol, and anti-gas medicine. Keep the basket—out of reach of small children—in the living area you use most, such as the family room, and you won't have to go to the nursery every time the baby needs a diaper change. This tip is especially helpful if the baby's room is upstairs.

Designate a Baby Drawer in the Kitchen

Assign a kitchen drawer for just baby stuff. Use it to store bottles, plastic inserts, bottle nipples, a bottle brush, baby spoons, breast pump, and pacifiers. To keep everything tidy, organize the baby drawer with inexpensive drawer dividers purchased from the kitchen organizer section of your discount department store.

Have a Toy Holder for the Car

Fill a clear Rubbermaid or other shoebox size plastic container with a few small baby toys and keep the box in your car near the driver's seat. When the baby gets fussy or just wants to play, you can easily hand him a toy. Be sure to keep extra pacifiers in this box. You may use any kind of container, but I like to use plastic so I can occasionally disinfect it. Every once in a while, check under seats and around car for "missing" toys!

Store Baby Food Items Together

I love using double rack Lazy Susan spice carousels to store jars of baby food. Also, baby supply stores sell plastic shelving designed to store baby food jars. The key to organizing baby food is to store it all together. Designate a shelf or cabinet for baby food only. Include baby cereal boxes, juices, formula, baby biscuits, and the like.

Organize "To Grow Into" Clothes

If you are fortunate enough to have a generous family member or friend who gives you "to grow into" clothes for your baby, you need to organize them. I like new boxes to store "to grow into" clothes. The best are brown corrugated boxes with no printing on them. I have also used cardboard filing boxes from office supply stores for storing clothes. Using a thick, black, permanent marker, clearly label the contents of each box.

You can organize clothes by size or by type. For example, when organizing clothes by size, you may mark them "12–24 months." When organizing by type, you might mark them "pants" or "summer clothes." It truly depends on what you have and what makes more sense to you. Store the boxes on the top shelf of your baby's closet with labels facing out. You won't forget what you have and they will be accessible as your little one grows.

Organize "Grow Out Of" Clothes

As your child grows out of his clothes, you can give them away to a thrift store or an organization's rummage sale, allowing you a tax deduction, consign them to make extra money, store them as keepsakes, or hand them down to younger siblings. There will also be clothes that will go directly in the trash! For clothes you are going to give away, use any box marked "giveaway" and store it on the top of your baby's closet. As soon as you know that a particular article of clothing will no longer fit your baby, put it in the "giveaway" box. Also box up all clothes you plan on consigning or selling at a garage sale.

When storing keepsake clothes, I prefer using plastic containers with tightly-sealed lids. Outside the box, attach a label that identifies the contents. You can store the container in the basement, attic, or any out-of-the-way place. For clothes you want to hand down to other children, organize them the same way you would "to grow into" clothes—either by type or by size.

Store Keepsake Items in a Special Box

Make a special box to store precious keepsakes for your child.

Make a special box for your child to store all precious keepsakes. Invest in a large plastic container— the Rubbermaid "Roughneck" 18-gallon is a good size and comes in a variety of colors. Using a thick black permanent marker, write "_____'s special box" (fill in the name of your child) on two sides of the container. Store all those special things you want to save: the blanket he was wrapped in when he was born, special cards from relatives, the signed baseball . . . you get the picture. My sons love to spend time occasionally looking through their special boxes; it reassures them that they are loved and reminds them of some of their happiest times.

CHAPTER 6

Kitchens

MOST PEOPLE THINK THAT the kitchen is where Mom belongs and where Mom should do all the work. But by encouraging children to be part of the kitchen activity, we create opportunities to teach them many lessons about order and responsibility. Make your kitchen kid-friendly by creating special places in the kitchen for the stuff kids use. If your kitchen is organized in a way that makes it easy for kids to help themselves, life will be easier for you!

For example, to help keep children from running under and around you while you are cooking, store silverware in the drawer closest to the eating area. When little ones want to set the table or if they just need a spoon, this arrangement will help to separate work activities and make food preparation less hectic.

Think "convenience" when setting up your kitchen, and group like things together. When every item has a home, your children will know where things belong and you will not be bombarded with questions about where items are. When they help you empty the dishwasher, they will know exactly where things go and will take pride in their ability to put things away properly. Let your kitchen be a place where your family can enjoy wonderful meals and good times together!

The following suggestions are easy ways to help make your kitchen kid-friendly.

CLEAN OUT JUNK DRAWERS

Most of you dread cleaning out junk drawers, but it will be worth the effort. Once you go through all the junk, you will realize that most of it is just that . . . *junk!* Throw it away.

There will be things that you will need to keep such as change, coupons, batteries, keys, and film. Find new spots for some of these items. Get an index box for coupons and store it on top of the refrigerator. As soon as you clip them, put your coupons in the box. Use a small wicker basket or bowl on the counter to hold change.

Then, keep one drawer for those necessary miscellaneous things that usually get thrown in the junk drawers. If you had a specific place for these things, they would not have ended up in a junk drawer in the first place! To keep things separated, organize your new miscellaneous drawer with dividers or small plastic baskets. Try to keep it neat and orderly so that you can find things easily.

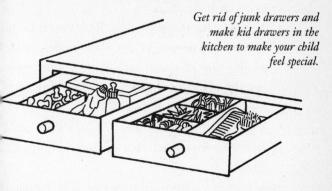

Get rid of junk drawers and make kid drawers in the kitchen to make your child feel special.

CREATING KID DRAWERS

The purpose of cleaning out junk drawers is to make kid drawers. These will be drawers used only for kids' things.

- A drawer for kids' cups, cup seals, and special straws. Toddlers will feel proud to get their own cup to bring to Mommy when they are thirsty.
- A drawer for bottles, nipples, pacifiers, and other miscellaneous baby stuff. When the baby is crying, it will be nice to know exactly where to find that much-needed pacifier!

- A drawer for paper cups, paper plates, plastic utensils, and napkins. Sometimes it's nice not to worry about cleaning up the dishes. Let your kids help themselves to a snack. Train them to throw away their paper goods as soon as they are finished.
- A drawer for playing cards, flash cards, small puzzles, and games. When your children want to play any of these games, they will know exactly where to find it and where to put it back when they are finished.
- A drawer for special treats. Stock your children's favorite snacks for them to help themselves.
- A drawer for first-aid items such as bandage strips, peroxide, antibiotic cream, thermometer, and cough drops. You'll be able to soothe a "boo-boo" in a flash. (Always install a childproof drawer lock to keep little ones from getting into medicines.)
- A drawer for school supplies: ruled paper, pencils, and rulers. Your children will always be prepared to do their homework.
- A drawer for arts and crafts items: coloring books, construction paper, stickers, markers, crayons, scissors, and glue sticks. Have your

little artist make you a masterpiece while you cook dinner.

- A drawer for your little girl's hair things: bows, barrettes, ribbons, clips, a water spray bottle, hair brush, comb. When you're running late, it will be handy to have everything all together.

- A drawer for thank-you notes, personalized stationery, address labels with your child's name, fun stamps, and pens. Children are never too young to learn the value of sending thank-you notes.

HANG A LARGE CALENDAR ON THE REFRIGERATOR

Write all important dates on the calendar as soon as you make an appointment, get an invitation, or realize you need to accomplish some task by a deadline. Talk to your children about the importance of writing down important events so that we don't forget them. Use examples that affect them personally, such as "Collin, let's write down your gymnastics class on the calendar so Mommy can see you do the jellyroll!"

Train older children to write all their important dates on the calendar. Have them use a pencil, and teach them not to take up all the space on that day.

Establishing this habit in their early years will help them learn principles of time management.

Write your menus on the calendar too. Children can then look forward to the good things they will have for dinner.

INVEST IN MAGNETIC PAPER HOLDERS

Everyone who has been in my kitchen loves these! Each of my sons has his own box attached to the refrigerator for his special papers. They can be purchased in the kitchen organizational department in stores such as Target, K-Mart, or The Container Store.

I used a paint pen to write "Cameron's Papers" and "Collin's Papers" on each of their boxes. We all know that this is where to put baseball schedules, classroom papers, church activity notices, school directories, and the like. This holder is just for their papers so it's easy for them to find what they need.

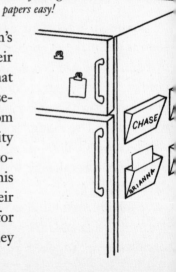

Magnetic paper holders make finding all the papers easy!

These boxes are also ideal for storing take-out menus and pizza coupons. You can even make a "Mom's Papers" holder for yourself.

Organize School Lunch Boxes

Make a place for your children's lunch boxes or bags. You might choose a cabinet, drawer, or shelf, or decide to hang them on a hook. Make it easy for little ones to get out their own box or bag and return it when they come home.

Select a shelf or basket specifically for lunch box snacks. Train your children to pick their snack every morning (or the evening before) and put it in their lunch box. Help them eat healthful snacks by providing fruits and veggies washed and ready to go.

Designate a specific place in the refrigerator for drink boxes and allow children to choose a drink for their lunch box.

If your child uses a thermal bottle, store it in the lunch box so that it is always ready to go. When your child is old enough, allow him to pour his own drink into the bottle.

Make the lunch box your child's responsibility. As soon as he comes home from school, train him to dispose of any trash left in the box, put plasticware or reusable items in the sink, and put the ice pack back into the freezer.

HANG A BULLETIN BOARD NEAR THE KITCHEN PHONE

Write important phone numbers on index cards and tack them on the bulletin board. Make an index card for emergency numbers and include your home phone, car phone, beeper, and address. This information will help baby-sitters as well as your children in case of emergency.

Make an index card for each child and list any important numbers that relate just to that child—school numbers, friends' numbers, bus number, etc.

If you are divorced or separated from the child's other parent, make a card that includes all phone numbers and the address where the other parent can be reached.

Make a card with neighbors' phone numbers.

For young children who can't yet read, attach photographs or pictures next to important phone numbers. For example, next to "911" paste a picture of a fire truck, ambulance, or police car.

HANG A KEY HOLDER

Make life simp[le] by having a place to hang [keys.]

Attach an identifying tag to each key ("pool," "tennis courts," "bike lock," etc.). Teach your children to return each key promptly after they have used it. Train your-self to keep your keys there too!

HANG A CHORE CHART

Use a bulletin board, chalk board, erase board, or cardboard—whatever works for you. Have a family meeting and discuss the division of chores. Let your kids decide which chores each wants to do so long as it's fair for everybody.

Choose a reward for doing assigned tasks. It may be praise or extra allowance, but realize that the key to success with any chore chart involves consistency and follow-through. It is very important to teach a young child that he is an important member of the family and that each member has a responsibility to help take care of their home.

OTHER KITCHEN IDEAS

- Let your child help you prepare a meal. This activity teaches children the importance of assembling various items for food preparation and taking each step in a logical order. Choose a time when you are unhurried and have extra time to be patient with his efforts. Children love to measure, mix, and pour, so encourage your child to participate in as much of the work as is appropriate for his age. He will feel proud of his accomplishment!

- Ask for your child's help in making out the grocery list. Ask her to look through the cabinets and refrigerator to see what items are needed. Explain to her that you will buy only what is on the list. Then, if your child asks for special items during shopping time, remind her that you are buying just the things on the list. Be patient but firm, and she will soon understand the rules.

- Ask for your children's help in making out daily menus for the upcoming week. Not only will they feel important for having been consulted, they will be far more likely to eat the food that they themselves have suggested. To make them feel extra special, plan a night for each child to have his or her favorite meal.

- Purchase a hanging organizer for brooms and mops and hang it in the pantry or laundry room. Then buy a kid-sized broom and hang it on a low hook next to yours. Your toddler can feel important when he helps Mommy clean up, and older kids will have no excuse for not sweeping their own clutter.

- Tupperware is a favorite kitchen toy for babies. If you are lucky enough to have a large, deep, low drawer in your kitchen, store your Tupperware (or other plastic containers) there. Use a large square container to hold all the lids, and everything will be together and within easy reach for both you and baby. If you do not have a suitable drawer for plastic containers, store them in large, clear containers inside a cabinet, or put them in a small, square laundry basket in the pantry. You can pull the basket out onto the floor for baby to play with.

- Use large, clear plastic containers for your children's cereal. Cut out the names from the box of cereals you purchase regularly, and paste one on each container. Select containers with flip-top lids for easy pouring and resealing. These containers also keep out bugs.

- Make it easy for your child to take telephone messages. Begin by teaching your child the proper way to answer the phone and practice with him on a toy phone or unplugged phone. Fill a wicker basket with pads, sticky notes, or index cards and place it next to the phone along with pens and pencils. One of my favorite kitchen organizers is a pretty cream pitcher filled with pencils and placed next to a basket of writing pads.

Make it convenient for children to take a telephone message.

- The most effective way to train a child to be organized in the kitchen is for Mom and Dad to keep it that way. Be a great role model and your child will follow your example!

CHAPTER 7

EntryWays

HAVE YOU EVER BEEN running late for an appointment and couldn't find your keys? Or spent a harried morning looking for your child's misplaced backpack? Or mislaid your purse?

If you can relate to any of these situations, you will understand why it's important to organize your entryway. Your entryway could be your front door, back door, laundry room, or mudroom—whatever area through which you enter and exit your home. If you can provide specific places at the entryway for such things as keys, purses, children's shoes, and backpacks, you can eliminate those frantic last-minute searches when leaving the house.

Organize your entry-ways and exits so that coats, shoes, backpacks, and so on have a place to go.

Listed below are ideas for places to put all the stuff we need to keep handy by the doorway.

ROUND UP SCATTERED SHOES

One of the biggest complaints I hear from clients is that there are too many shoes scattered around the entryway. Most often the problem exists because there is simply no designated place to put shoes, so kids (and adults) kick them off and leave them anywhere!

One of my favorite shoe containers for the entryway is a large square wicker basket. I've also used long decorative planters from a garden shop. Any similar container will work—the only require-ment is that it must be big enough and sturdy enough to hold your family's shoes.

Place the shoe container in a logical and conven-ient place near your entryway. When your container starts overflowing, have your kids (adults too!) return their extra shoes to their closets. Each of my boys has his own shoe basket. Since they were old enough to carry their own shoes, I have trained them to put their shoes into their proper baskets.

An alternative is to use shoe racks or shelves. Again, choose something that fits your space and that will accommodate the number of shoes that accumulate. The point is to *have a place* for shoes. The easier you make it for everyone to put their shoes there, the more likely it is they will do it.

An added bonus to training your children to remove their shoes when they enter the house is that it helps to keep carpets and floors clean longer, which means less mopping and vacuuming for you or for them.

CORRAL COATS AND JACKETS

For your entryway, consider using hook bars with *lots* of hooks on them, similar to the ones teachers use in the classroom. You can find decorative hook bars in catalogs, department stores, and in discount stores like Marshall's and T.J. Maxx. Make sure to hang the bar low enough so that your children can hang up their own coats without help.

Hang all of your children's coats (windbreaker, parka, raincoat, etc.) on a hook bar and it will be easy for them to choose the coat appropriate for the weather.

STASH YOUR WINTER STUFF

Designate a place for everyone's gloves, hats, and scarves. If your child knows there is a spot for her mittens to go, she will more likely put them there when she comes inside. Then she can find *both* of them when she is ready to go outside again. I use a square picnic basket placed on a shelf near our entry door. Any container will do; just place it somewhere handy.

CONSIDER AN UMBRELLA STAND

I love pretty umbrella stands! If you have at least two umbrellas with long handles, you might want to invest in an umbrella stand and place it near your entryway. If you're like me and have the kind with a short handle, hang it on a hook next to your raincoat.

DON'T FORGET NOTES AND REMINDERS

Having some sort of message board (bulletin or erase board) hanging in sight as you are leaving the house is a big help for important reminders. You can leave notes like "bring lunch box" or "PTA meeting tonight." Encourage your children to write their own messages on the message board when they need last-minute reminders.

HANG UP YOUR KEYS

Having a key holder is good for your sanity! Train yourself and your kids to hang your keys on a key rack *as soon as you walk in the door*. It's great to always know where your keys are! You can purchase a decorative key holder or just attach key hooks directly on the wall near the entry door. I screwed several hooks in the bottom of my bulletin board for my keys.

DESIGNATE A SPOT FOR HANDBAGS

Designate a spot for your handbag, and put it there as soon as you come in the door. You might choose a bedroom shelf, a closet hook, or a drawer somewhere handy. My purse hangs on a pretty blue wooden peg bar in the kitchen.

HAVE A SPOT FOR THE DOG LEASH

Make it easy to take your pup for a walk. I hang my sweet Lhasa Apso's leash on the same bar with my purse. If your child knows where your dog's leash is, she can take out the dog quickly when needed.

CREATE A SPECIAL PLACE FOR YOUR CHILD'S STUFF

I have always made a special place in our entryway for my boys' things. Each child has his own shoe basket and a rack on which to hang his coat, backpack, and umbrella. Each rack is placed appropriately for each child's individual height with a bulletin board hung above to display school art. Using a paint pen, I wrote "Cameron's Art" and "Collin's Art" on top of each bulletin board. I also have a small chair placed next to each of the boy's areas so each has a convenient place to sit when taking shoes on and off.

Another thing you might store in your child's "area" is his musical instrument. If your child is unable to leave his instrument at school, having it handy in a routine place will help him to remember to take it to school on band day.

TAKE ONE LAST LOOK

Hang a mirror near your door. Choose one long enough so your little ones can use it too. Remind everyone to take one last look before school to see if there is any toothpaste on their face! Make this family mirror special by using a paint pen to write something on it that will make your family smile.

CHAPTER 8

Toys, Hobbies, and Sports Items

THIS CHAPTER DEALS WITH the bulk of your child's stuff. But before I begin giving tips for each category, I would like to talk about the benefits of choosing *quality* toys rather than a *quantity* of toys. I've seen a lot of children's bedrooms in my job, and it amazes me how much stuff some kids have. I feel very confident in saying that children who have a vast hoard of toys have forgotten about most of their stuff, play with only a small fraction of their things, and truly value very little of it.

Take a good look at your child's room (and your checkbook) and decide if your child has way too much stuff. Ask yourself if you think your child appreciates all that he has. Does he take care of his things? Does she play with most of her toys? If you feel your child has far too much, it's time to weed out unused items.

When shopping for toys, choose a few good quality items rather than a lot of cheaply made trinkets. A set of wooden blocks is a good example of a quality toy. I purchased wooden blocks when my older son was a toddler. Back then, the blocks helped him with coordination and balance; now, at age ten, he builds forts with them. If you choose well-made toys that have a relatively long life span, your child will get more play value for the money you spend. Be a good steward of your money, and your child will learn from your example.

Toys

Add to Collections

A collection is usually meaningful to children because they get excited about adding new pieces and watching it grow. My son Collin loves his toy collections! He collects plastic bugs, animals, cars and trucks, *Toy Story* figures, *Lion King* figures, G.I. Joe figures, Beanie Babies, and army men. Collections help children develop their creativity. Collections also teach kids to appreciate and value their toys.

Separate Toys and Collections

Use containers to separate different kinds of toys and toy collections. Clear plastic containers are best for toys that will be stacked on shelves. Just be sure to label each container clearly so that the contents can be easily identified.

Make a Home for Toys

After toys are separated and labeled, find a home for them. If your child knows that each toy (or collection of toys) has a designated place, he will know where to find it and know where to put it away.

Empty Out Toy Boxes

I discussed toy boxes in Chapter 2, but I will restate my philosophy here. Toy boxes usually get filled with a bunch of junk, and it becomes difficult for a child to find the particular toy he wants. Toy boxes are like junk drawers—they usually overflow with too much stuff that doesn't belong there.

Begin organizing the toy box by emptying it out completely. Throw away any trash and broken toys. Train your child not to put miscellaneous toys in the toy box as they will be too hard to find. Instead, choose a collection of larger toys to go in the toy box, such as baby dolls only or stuffed animals only.

Gather Up Sand Toys

For sand toys, I love using big net bags with pull cords; they're light, easy to carry, and you can just shake out the sand. Keep all sand toys in one container so you will always be ready to head to the park or beach for some sand fun.

Go Through Toys Often

Children are children, and toys will get misplaced and broken. Every month or so, spend some time going through your child's toys. Work with your child to put misplaced toys back in their homes. Throw out broken toys, games, and puzzles that have missing pieces.

Play with One Game at a Time

Train kids to put away one game before pulling out another. I don't want fanatical children who don't know how to relax and have fun, but neither do I want my children to tear apart a room with every toy and game they have and then be completely frustrated trying to clean it up. Teach your children that it's a lot easier to clean up if you do it as you go along.

If your child has a friend who destroys your child's room every time he comes over to play, set some rules. Tell your child's friend that your family treats your property with respect and if he wants to play at your house, he will have to do the same. Kids appreciate rules and will obey them if they know what the rules are.

Stash Some Toys for Awhile

Sometimes putting several toys away for a while and then bringing them out later will give them new life. It's almost as though a much-loved friend has returned. If your child has lost interest in a particular toy or game, put it away for awhile.

Let Kids Do the Clean-Up

Too often we do things for our children that they should do for themselves. There are too many lazy children in this world! Work is a part of life, and even young children should learn to work. Teach your children to pick up after themselves—it's good for them!

HOBBIES

Having a hobby is a positive thing, because it shows that your child is dedicated and goal-oriented. The best way we can support and encourage our children's hobbies is to provide the things needed for those hobbies. A child's hobby may not interest us, but it is important to the child. Let your child know you are proud of him for the things he accomplishes.

If your son likes to build model airplanes, make sure to have extra model glue and paints on hand. To make him feel special, install shelves or a shelving unit in his room to display his planes.

If your daughter likes creating jewelry with beads, purchase an organizing container for her beads. While you are shopping, keep an eye out for unusual or fun beads and save them as gifts for her on special occasions.

Make your child feel special by making special displays for his or her collectibles and hobbies.

SPORTS ITEMS

Participating in sports is a terrific thing for your child because of the physical exercise it provides, as well as many other benefits.

One way to encourage your kids is to provide a place to keep all their sports items. To organize the space effectively, separate items according to sports so that your child can find the items he or she needs. Below is a list of ideas for organizing sports items:

- If you have a lot of sports items, you will need large containers in your garage to sort the various equipment. Have a container for baseball stuff only, tennis stuff only, balls only, water sports stuff only, etc.

- Designate a shelf in your garage for sports-related shoes such as golf shoes, baseball-foot-ball-soccer cleats, hiking boots, rollerblades, biking shoes, etc. Designate a container to hold all protective gear for rollerblading or biking. Keep all helmets together as well. Either put them on a shelf or place a hook bar nearby to keep them within easy reach.

- Use a large net bag (with pull string) to hold all scuba- or skin-diving equipment.

- If you have a lot of camping equipment, purchase a large plastic container (with lid and wheels) to store all your supplies. Take it camping with you, and use it to keep items dry. Having all your camping equipment together reduces stress while planning this wonderful family activity.

- Keep air pumps handy for rafts, bikes, and balls. Keep extra needles on hand to blow up balls. They are little and get lost easily.
- Keep sunscreen and bug repellent handy by designating a container for it in the garage.
- Organize your family's bikes in the garage. My dream is to have one of those bike racks like they have at my boys' school. Another idea is to hang bikes from the garage ceiling or wall. Make it easy to get to your kids' bikes. Train your kids to keep their bikes in the area you have chosen, so that parents don't stumble over them trying to get to the tools!
- Have a designated spot in your child's bedroom for all sports clothing (jersey's, hats, socks, shin guards, etc.) It can be very frustrating when your child can't find his jersey and he has a game in an hour.
- Make a special shelf for all your children's trophies so they can feel proud of their accomplishments! Use a bulletin board to display any recognition patches or awards.
- Buy a really big blue container (the color of water) and place it in the garage to store floats, goggles, fins, water toys, and life preservers. When summer ends, store it in the basement.

CHAPTER 9

Mom's Taxi

IF YOU SPEND AS much time driving as I do, then you probably feel as though your car is your second home! Since parents spend a lot of time driving kids here and there, we might as well have a well-organized car to make the driving experience as peaceful as possible. Here are some great suggestions to make "Mom's taxi" a fun and efficient way to travel!

CLEAN IT OUT!

Before you can organize your car, take a little time to clean out all the accumulated stuff. Get a big empty box or laundry hamper and transfer everything from the car to the container. Cleaning the car completely means emptying the glove compartment, the ashtrays, the seat pockets—everything. Take the container to a comfortable spot and go through the contents. Throw out the trash, return any items that belong inside the house, and put aside all the things that you want to keep in the car. We'll talk later about what to do with stuff you want to keep for the car.

Now that the car is cleaned out, the next step is to clean it up. Who doesn't love driving around in a really clean car! If you can afford it, take it to an auto detail-wash-dry place. If you choose to do the job yourself, wash the outside, vacuum the carpet, and wipe the interior hard surfaces with furniture polish. If you have a child who is old enough, you might entice him or her to help you by offering a couple of dollars. Once your car is cleared of junk and dirt, consider some of the following ideas for storing stuff and making your "taxi" kid-friendly!

Keeping a toy container on t floor of the back seat will he keep toys from scattering.

GET A TOY BOX

Kids who travel in our van love our toy container. It's inevitable that toys will end up in the car, so why not keep them from scattering? You

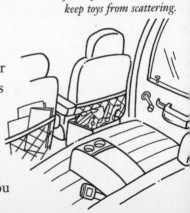

don't need a very large container, just one big enough to hold a few books and small toys. Use any type of plastic container without holes so that small toy parts will not escape. (Also, a solid container is easier to clean and disinfect.) Your kids will love having a toy box in the car!

HAVE ACTIVITIES AVAILABLE FOR OLDER KIDS

Kids just want to have fun, no matter what their age. When you do a lot of city driving or take driving vacations, have some activities available for the older ones. If your kids love to draw, travel with a sketchpad, markers, and colored pencils. Other ideas include crossword puzzles, magazines or educational books, and portable electronic games. Find or create a place in the car to keep these items; seat pockets work well.

MAKE A MOM BOX

I love my mom box! It's filled with things I like to have handy while away from home, such as a box of tissues, antibacterial wipes, a few Band-Aids, my favorite lotion, aspirin or other pain reliever, a small makeup bag filled with a travel-sized sewing kit, dental floss, nail clippers and file, small scissors, and a lipstick. I also have a leather zippered pouch for restaurant and store coupons. I've found that when I keep them handy, I actually use them!

Organize Mom's taxi with everything you need.

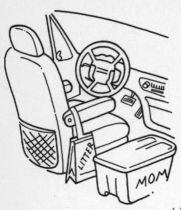

Since I drive a van, I place my mom box right next to me between the two front seats. If your car is a sedan, you might put your mom box on the floor on the front passenger side, or perhaps in the passenger seat if your kids usually ride in the back. The key is to have some accessible area in your car to place the things you would like to have while traveling. With a mom box, you'll always be prepared.

CREATE AN EFFICIENT GLOVEBOX

Just like kitchen drawers, a car's glove compartment frequently gets filled with junk. Clean it out and make it really useful. Here are some ideas that might work for you.

- Use it to hold extra napkins, straws, toothpicks, salt packets, and sugar and coffee creamer packages you get from fast-food restaurants. Then, when you fail to get any of these items, you will have your own backup supply.
- Make it your first-aid box.

- Turn it into a snack storage box. Fill with small packages of crackers, cookies, dried fruit, trail mix, and the like.
- Keep it supplied with notepads and pens.
- Store maps and travel guides.
- Store office supplies such as envelopes, stamps, Scotch tape, small stapler, scissors, and deposit envelopes for your bank and credit union.

GET A TRASH HOLDER

A variety of car trash holders are available in the auto accessory department of all discount stores. Mine is a folding vinyl bag with a strap that hangs on the arm of my seat. If anything spills inside the bag, the vinyl material prevents leaks. My friend Anna uses a medium-sized oval trash basket placed between the two front seats of her van. The point is to find a functional trash holder so that your kids' trash doesn't end up all over the car. Your trash container can be something as simple as a plastic grocery bag that hangs somewhere in the car. Be consistent about keeping it, and empty it often.

PLACE A SMALL LAUNDRY BASKET IN THE TRUNK OR REAR OF THE CAR

A small laundry basket is a great place to put wet suits, towels, or extra clothing. It also works well to keep miscellaneous items from rolling around in the back of the car and can serve as a carryall for items that need to be taken from car to house. Another great idea is to fill your basket with "a fun day at the park" stuff such as a ball, Frisbee, picnic blanket, tablecloth, and bubbles. Always be prepared to enjoy some spontaneous fun with your kids!

HIDE AN EXTRA KEY UNDER THE CAR

How many times have you locked yourself out of your car? Being locked out is always inconvenient and frustrating. If you have a key hidden somewhere under your car, you'll be back on the road in a jiffy. Hardware and auto supply stores sell small metal boxes designed just for this purpose. The boxes have superstrong magnetic backings that won't let go until you pull firmly on them. Simply place an extra key inside the box and attach it under the car well out of sight. Before I stashed my extra key, I always worried about locking myself out while my baby was inside the car—but that's never a concern anymore!

MAKE A SNACK BOX

My friend Debbie gave me this tip. Her son has hypoglycemia, so she always keeps some sort of snack handy for him when he needs a blood sugar boost. She keeps an insulated bag filled with all kinds of prepackaged snacks, along with some fruit or juice. Since all kids get snack attacks now and then, this idea is helpful for everyone and will help save money too. Your goodie box will cost less than a fast-food stop and, in addition, will allow you to supply more nutritious snacks to your children.

CHAPTER 10

Keepsakes

THERE ARE TIMES IN our children's lives that are so precious we want the memory to last forever. Every time I look at my boys' hospital baby blankets, memories of their births come flooding back. I get tears in my eyes when I think of the joy I felt holding my swaddled babies. Those blankets are very special to me, and I would never want to lose them. Since my boys and I have a number of keepsakes we want to keep safe, I've created a "Special Box" for each of us to keep these important keepsakes.

The key to preserving keepsakes is to designate a spot for them. When you put things here and there you're likely to forget where they are, and you can't really enjoy them. So, instead of shoving special cards in dresser drawers and tooth fairy teeth in your makeup drawer, it's best to have a certain place for all your children's special keepsakes.

I recommend storing keepsakes in plastic containers rather than in cardboard boxes. One of my clients had a flood in her basement, and her family's irreplaceable keepsakes were completely ruined. If they had been protected in plastic containers, they would not have been lost. Don't learn the hard way!

SECURE KEEPSAKES IN "SPECIAL BOXES"

As I mentioned earlier, "special boxes" are containers designated to hold all of your child's very special stuff. My boys love to look through their special boxes. We don't put a lot of junk in there—it's only for meaningful keepsakes they will always treasure. It's where we keep the baby blankets, letters and cards from relatives and friends, special pictures, awards, locks of baby hair, signed baseballs, the sweater Nanny knitted, and other important items.

You can start with a fairly small container, but eventually you will have to switch to a larger box as your children accumulate more treasures. When you need a bigger box, you might consider using a wooden toy box, cedar chest, or footlocker.

STORE PHOTOS IN PICTURE BOXES

These boxes are great! Designed for storing developed pictures, they are made of cardboard and come in a variety of colors and designs. They also come with index cards that are terrific for dividing and organizing your pictures. For example, when you file pictures of your child's birthday party, write "Katie's 6th birthday" on the index card. For Christmas pictures, write "Christmas 1999."

In our picture box I have special sections for Cameron and Collin. I labeled one index card with each of my boys' names, then filed pictures of each child in his own section. I have to admit that the stacks are pretty thick, but the boys *love* looking at pictures of themselves! Picture boxes are a great source for a picture when a teacher asks for one or when you are gathering material for a collage. From time to time, you will want to transfer each child's stack of pictures into his own photo album.

CREATE MEMORIES WITH SCRAPBOOKS

As parents, we want our children to know how very special and loved they are. One Christmas I made my boys their very own scrapbooks. I started with their newborn pictures and went through the years to the present. Beside each item in the book I wrote a line or two that related to that memento or picture. They loved this gift! After looking through his scrapbook, my oldest son remarked, "I have a lot of people who love me." Several companies and retail stores help you organize wonderful scrapbooks as well as provide the materials needed to help protect photos.

CHERISH KEEPSAKE CLOTHES

We all have precious little baby clothes that we want to keep forever. You probably can't give away your baby's christening gown or the outfit he wore home from the hospital. How about your little girl's first recital tutu? Your child will have some very special clothes that you will want to preserve as keepsakes.

Make a container just for storing and protecting these mementos. Before placing each item in the box, wrap it in a special tissue paper that preserves textiles (you can find it in organizing specialty stores). Make sure the clothing is clean and folded neatly before you put it in your keepsake container.

CARE FOR KEEPSAKE JEWELRY

Baby rings, their first cross, their Boy Scout ring—these special jewelry items will be lifelong treasures. Keep them safe in a small jewelry box stored in your child's special box.

BUY A "SCHOOL DAYS" BOOK

Many mail-order catalogs, such as *Walter Drake*, sell a book called "School Days" that holds all your child's report cards. There is also a page for each grade with designated places for a school picture and some information about that year. These books are well designed, colorful, and very inexpensive. Your children will treasure this remembrance of their childhood years.

MAKE THE MOST OF YOUR CHILD'S MASTERPIECES

We get a lot of art from our children. Some you'll throw away, but some you'll want to keep. Protect those precious masterpieces in a plastic container. I have found that the best size is the under-the-bed storage box.

My favorite thing to do with special pictures is to frame them and hang them in our home. There is nothing that makes my boys feel so proud of their work as seeing it displayed on our walls.

CHAPTER 11

Maintaining the Order

BY NOW I HOPE you are totally motivated to set up some organizational systems for your child. You have a bit of work ahead, but the results will be worth the effort! If you become overwhelmed with the number of changes you want to make, just remember that everything doesn't have to be done all at once. Tackle one area at a time and visualize the finished project. As you work, think of all the benefits your children will receive when you bring order to their lives.

We know *why* we need to organize our kids, and we've talked about the importance of a positive attitude. Now let's talk about how to maintain the order. Listed below are tips on helping our kids *stay* organized.

USE PRAISE

Praise your child every time she is orderly. Let her know how much you appreciate her being such a great help in caring for your home.

BE CONSISTENT

When you set up a new system, you must stick with it to make it really work for you. Consistency is especially important in the first few weeks after you change things around. Even though it might be really hard at first, a determined effort is crucial when you are trying to change your old disorganized self into a new creation. Keep at it! The rewards will come.

It may seem that *getting* organized is nothing but work, but you'll soon find out that *being* organized saves work!

EXPECT SUCCESS

Your child is likely to live up to your expectations, so give him attainable goals and allow him to reach them. Children love to make us proud, and we should give them this opportunity often. Don't rob them of the chance to be successful by doing for them what they can do for themselves. Believe in your child, and he will believe in himself.

On the flip side, don't be obsessive or overwhelm your child with expectations. Be careful not to be too critical of her, either. Remember that she is a child and sometimes it will take repeated efforts for her to learn new things. Explain *clearly* what your expectations are so that there will be no misunderstanding. You child wants to please you—she just needs to know what you expect from her.

You may also have to accept the fact that your child may never meet *your* expectations. As a parent of a special needs child, I learned this lesson from personal experience. When Collin was a baby, I was angry that he was not able to do the things that other children his age could do. I asked God why Collin had to struggle so hard to achieve every milestone in his development. He let me know that the struggle was actually *mine*. I was not accepting my son exactly the way God intended him to be. Now I have learned to treasure Collin's unique gifts as I watch him succeed at his own pace and in his own way.

Every child is unique. Discover your child's personality and choose goals together that will enable your child to achieve success.

PROVIDE RESPONSIBILITIES

We have talked about how important it is for a child to feel that she is an important member of the family. By giving her *responsibilities and rewards*, we let her know how vital she is to the family unit. Let your child have her own age-appropriate responsibilities. When you commit yourself to raising a responsible child, you will be amazed at how much she can accomplish.

We live in a society filled with lazy, irresponsible children. The more we do for them, the less they do for themselves. Who should take the blame? You can give your child an advantage by teaching him the importance of work. Then, have some fun—hard work deserves rewards. When a child finishes a job, celebrate!

GIVE CONSEQUENCES

A smart parent will give their children consequences when they don't follow the rules. You and your children need to talk together about expectations and consequences. They deserve to know exactly what is expected of them, and what the consequences will be if they choose to disobey.

For example, if you want your child to put away his toys before dinner, explain to him exactly what he must do and what the consequences will be if he doesn't follow the rule. Be specific. Tell him that he must pick up all his toys and put them in the proper container before he comes to dinner. Be sure that he understands that there can't be any toys left out.

Tell him that if you find anything left out of place, you will take that toy, and he will not be able to play with it for two days (or whatever time seems appropriate). When you make the expectations and the consequences very clear to him, he will quickly learn the value of following rules.

Someone once told me that she makes her children " buy" back anything they leave on the floor. Perhaps this idea might work for you!

Children want to feel that you care about what they do. But if there are no consequences for disobedience, your children fail to learn an important life lesson. They fail to learn they have choices in life, and that a good choice usually produces positive results while a poor choice generally leads to an undesirable outcome.

ORGANIZE EACH SPRING AND FALL

Just as you do spring cleaning, you need to do spring (and fall) organizing. Spring and fall are really the ideal times to organize your closets and drawers because most of us are changing our clothes with the seasons.

Remove what is no longer used. If your child has a pair of corduroy pants that are already snug when you do your spring organizing, don't save them for next fall. They won't fit. Tidy up your child's closet and drawers and make sure that everything is in the place you have designated. Go through your child's toys and discard any broken or unused items. In effect, reorganize twice a year! When you follow this routine, it will be easier to maintain order.

REMEMBER . . . YOU ARE A ROLE MODEL

Our children are constantly watching us. Scary thought, isn't it! What kind of attitude do you have? Do you want your child to model after you? If you have a cheerful attitude, it will rub off on your child!

How do you take care of your home? A great Bible truth in Proverbs 14:1 says that "The wise woman builds her house, but with her own hands the foolish one tears hers down." Are you wise or foolish? Do you take care of your home or do you let it get out of control? I am not suggesting that you keep your home like a *House Beautiful* photograph. We can all appreciate a beautifully decorated model home, but that image is impossible to maintain when you have children living there! The goal of an orderly home is to create a peaceful haven, not a perfect showplace.

God has given us moms an extraordinary role in the home. What we do with that role can dramatically affect the lives of our children. I can choose to feel guilty about the mistakes I make, or I can choose to focus on the impact I have on my precious boys. My choice is to look to God and allow him to make the best of me.

Remember that our children are in training with us. They are training to be responsible and caring adults. We are reminded in Proverbs 22:6 to "Train a child in the way he should go, and when he is old he will not turn from it."

FOCUS ON HOW BLESSED WE ARE!

As we close, focus on your role as a mom. Think about how lucky you are! I once heard someone say that being a mom is like being in a special club, and our children are the reward. As we continue to learn and grow to be the best moms we can be, never forget how truly blessed we are. As you strive to get your kids' stuff organized, keep in mind that everything we do for our children is a gift from our heart to theirs.

About This Busy Mom

LEIGH ROLLAR MINTZ IS a professional organizer and owner of Let Leigh Organize. She organizes homes and offices and also teaches workshops on simple ways to get kids organized. Her heartfelt desire is to encourage moms by showing them how to simplify their lives by bringing order into their homes. She lives in Alpharetta, Georgia, with her two sons, Cameron and Collin. To request speaking engagements contact her at:

Leigh Rollar Mintz
13331 Harpley Court
Alpharetta, Georgia 30004

Leighrollarmintz@AOL.com

Find out how MOPS International can help you become part of the MOPS©to©Mom Connection.

MOPS International
P.O. Box 102200
Denver, CO 80250-2200
Phone 1-800-929-1287 or 303-733-5353
E-mail: Info@MOPS.org
Web site: http://www.MOPS.org

To learn how to start a MOPS group,
call 1-888-910-MOPS.
For MOPS products call The MOPShop
1-888-545-4040.

Little Books for Busy Moms

Softcover 0-310-23514-6

Softcover 0-310-23511-1

Softcover 0-310-23513-8

Softcover 0-310-23515-4

MOTHERS OF
MⱯPS®
PRESCHOOLERS

Softcover 0-310-23659-2

Ready for Kindergarten

An Award-Winning Teacher's Plan to Prepare Your Child for School

By Sharon Wilkins

Filled with 156 fun activities designed to equip boys and girls for school success, this unique little book can show u how to help your child lay the foundation for devel-ing healthy friendships and a love for God. In addi-n, it can help you give your child a giant head start in ch core subjects as math, reading, science, art, and sic!

rough three simple, creative activities per week, you n laugh and play with your child while teaching impor-t skills. Let an award-winning kindergarten teacher th twenty-four years of classroom experience show w exciting activities—from making your initials out playdough to building a cardboard train out of boxes—n make your child *Ready for Kindergarten!*

Pick up your copy today at your local bookstore!

MOTHERS OF

MOPS®

PRESCHOOLERS

Hardcover 0-310-20097-0

What Every Mom Needs

Meet Your Nine Basic Needs (and Be a Better Mom)
Elisa Morgan & Carol Kuykendall

If you enjoyed *What Every Child Needs*, you'll love its be
ing companion! In *What Every Mom Needs*, Elisa Morg
Carol Kuykendall of MOPS International point the
relief and fulfillment in the midst of motherhood's
pace. After more than twenty years of research and e
ence with moms, MOPS has identified your nine basic
as a mother: significance, identity, growth, intimacy, in
tion, help, recreation, perspective, and hope. *What*
Mom Needs is an invaluable resource for women who long to expand their pe
horizons and become better mothers at the same time.

What Every Child Needs

Getting to the Heart of Mothering
Elisa Morgan & Carol Kuykendall

Elisa Morgan and Carol Kuykendall come together again!
This time Elisa and Carol detail in a warm and nurturing
style the nine needs of every child: security, affirmation,
family, respect, play, guidance, discipline, independence,
and hope. Don't miss the great stories, helpful hints, and
practical suggestions that will help you recognize and meet
these needs in the life of your child.

Hardcover 0-310-

Hardcover 0-310-22698-8

When Husband & Wife Become Mom & Da

What Every Marriage Needs
Elisa Morgan & Carol Kuyendall

Just when you thought you'd adjusted to each other
when you and your spouse had achieved a satisfying b
in your relationship—it happened. Your first child ar
Things have never been the same since . . . and they nev
be. So how do you regain your equilibrium now tha
have children?

Help is here! From open-hearted interviews with 1,00
moms and dads around the country *When Husband &*
Become Mom & Dad helps new parents and soon-to-be parents understand the
sition from husband and wife to mom and dad, and helps them establish the
dation for a fulfilling and vital marriage relationship.

MOTHERS OF MOPS PRESCHOOLERS

om's Devotional Bible

Hardcover 0-310-92501-0
Softcover 0-310-92422-7

ns, you don't have to go it
e! The *Mom's Devotional Bible*
companion and trusted
ce of wisdom to help you
g the path of mothering. A
year of weekday devotions
ten by Elisa Morgan, presi-
t of MOPS (Mothers of
choolers) International, are
bined with the Bible text to
r you and moms every-
re a fresh perspective on
cs such as time manage-
t, mentors for moms, sibling rivalry,
much more. And on weekends, find new insights as you
lore "special interest" areas like "A Mother's Legacy,"
in Up a Child," "A Time to Play," and "Get Growing!"

complete text of the best-selling New International Version
vides accuracy you can trust. A list of resources in the back
he Bible shows you where to turn for help with the special
llenges you face as a mother. And from family traditions
raying for young children, twenty full-color pages add a
m, keepsake touch. The *Mom's Devotional Bible*—get yours
ay!

wide selection of *Mom's Devotional Bible* gift products is
also available.

We want to hear from you. Please send your
comments about this book to us in care of the address
below. Thank you.

ZondervanPublishingHouse
Grand Rapids, Michigan

A Division of HarperCollinsPublishers